Beyond the Bottom Line

BEYOND THE BOTTOM LINE

Courtney C. Brown

Studies of the Modern Corporation
Graduate School of Business
Columbia University

MACMILLAN PUBLISHING CO., INC.
New York

Collier Macmillan Publishers
London

Macmillan Publishing Co., Inc.
866 Third Avenue, New York, N.Y. 10022

Collier Macmillan Canada, Ltd.

Library of Congress Catalog Card Number: 79–1954

Printed in the United States of America

printing number

1 2 3 4 5 6 7 8 9 10

Library of Congress Cataloging in Publication Data

Brown, Courtney C.
  Beyond the bottom line.

  (Studies of the modern corporation)
  Includes index.
  1. Industry--Social aspects. 2. Corporations.
I. Title. II. Series.
HD60.B76 1979   658.4'08   79-1954
ISBN 0-02-904660-2

STUDIES OF THE MODERN CORPORATION
Graduate School of Business, Columbia University

The Program for Studies of the Modern Corporation is devoted to the advancement and dissemination of knowledge about the corporation. Its publications are designed to stimulate inquiry, research, criticism, and reflection. They fall into three categories: works by outstanding businessmen, scholars, and professional men from a variety of backgrounds and academic disciplines; annotated and edited selections of business literature; and business classics that merit republication. The studies are supported by outside grants from private business, professional, and philanthropic institutions interested in the program's objectives.

RICHARD EELLS
Director

The Graduate School of Business
Columbia University
acknowledges with appreciation
a grant from
Gilman Paper Company
that has made this
publication possible

This book is dedicated to the many positive
opportunities available to the leaders
of the modern business corporation.

Contents

Preface   xv

Introduction   xix

Part I

*The Business Corporation
in the Modern World*

CHAPTER 1   The Business Corporation in Transition   3

Change Is Underway
Diminishing Public Approval
The Case for the Single Purpose Corporation
The Corporation's "Quasi-Constituencies"
Hazards to the Corporation and Society
Management's Dilemma
Public Policy Alternatives
Dual Influences of the Business Corporation

CHAPTER 2   Contrasting Social Values   16

Concepts that Shaped the Corporation
Centuries of Explosive Growth
Origins of the Current Dilemma
The Shifting Role of Government
Expanding Business Involvement
Employment and the Work Cycle

CONTENTS

Part II

Issues: Apparent and Real

CHAPTER 3   Apparent Issues   37

The Content of Economic Education
Quasi-Constituency Representation and
    Interlocking Boards
Stockholder Democracy
Ethical Conduct in an Immoral World

CHAPTER 4   Real Issues   63

Competition and Antitrust Policies
Inflation and the Pass-Through
Disciplining Competition

Part III

Organizing for Enlarged Responsibilities

CHAPTER 5   Authority Based on Consensus   81

Two Models of the Corporation: Small and Large
One-Man Direction vs. Group Consensus
Limitations on the Chief Executive Officer
A New Look at One-Man Control
A Strengthened Role for the Corporate Board
Composition of the Board

CHAPTER 6   Restructuring the Corporation   100

The Inadequacies of Government
The Characteristic Corporate Structure
Some General Features of Social Commitment
Modifying Administrative Structure

CHAPTER 7   Business-Government Relations   119

The Work of Government
The Work of Business
Joint Assignments

Contents

CHAPTER 8   Innovation Abroad   130

  The Spread of Global Investment
  Adjusting to the World Economy
  Adjusting to World Cultures and Politics
  Managerial Innovation

CHAPTER 9   Description: A Preface to Prescription   141

Bibliography   146

Index   153

Preface

As the manuscript for this book was readied for the publisher I realized that, apart from a quotation, the terms *capitalism* and *socialism* did not appear in the text. In retrospect, this may have been the result of a conviction that both terms, shop-worn and ambiguous, inaccurately describe the nature of contemporary economic institutions and business organizations. Or the omission may have been the result of an intuitive effort to avoid the use of concepts based on blueprints designed in years past and excessively charged with emotional content.

The attempt here is to explore as objectively as possible, the future implications of what appears to be a groundswell of change in the societal values that the public holds most important. More particularly, it is to delineate some of the alterations that may be imposed on the business corporation and its management by the addition, to the traditional single goal of making a profit, of what has come to be called *social responsibility*. It appears that modifications will be required (1) in the attitudes of business about itself and of the public about business, (2) in the background experience of those sharing in business decisions, (3) in the administrative structures of the corporation, and (4) in a redefinition of the functions of business and government and their relationships to each other.

That is a large order. Change is not comfortable. Policy choices available to corporate management all appear to be disagreeable, some more than others. That is the dilemma. Few will be happy with the prognostications made here, regardless of the place they occupy on the spectrum of political opinion—the business leader because these changes would require him to share his present authority and would obfuscate the clarity of his traditional goals, the critic of business who simply would not trust a shift of broadened responsibilities to business leaders, the government official whose reluctance to surrender power and influence is well known.

Yet the public insistence on moving quality-of-life considerations to center stage is proving hard to resist. When this desire is associated with a concomitant disillusionment with the capabilities of government and a resentment against the present levels of taxes, the pressure over time on the business corporation to extend its societal activities may be irresistible. Even though the process of change may be emotionally painful, the corporation in its probable future activities could have the opportunity of even greater public service than it has provided in the past in the form of material abundance.

It is interesting to reflect about where one's ideas may have originated. A part comes from reading, although I must confess to finding limited material that bears directly on the analytical substance of this book. There is, of course, much written that relates to the historical background of the corporation's development, and to the pros and cons of contemporary corporate practice. Here the attempt is to penetrate the misty outlines of its future.

A part of one's thoughts comes from extended discussions with associates and colleagues. My continuing association with the sharp and well-read minds of the faculty of the Graduate School of Business of Columbia University has been a resource of great value. My personal experience with senior assignments in the corporate world extending over several decades, however, has perhaps been the major contributor to the thoughts developed in these pages. Professor Melvin Anshen has been more than generous with his thoughts. My literary deficiencies have been compensated by the thorough editing of Chauncey G. Olinger, Jr. Appreciation is due also to Patricia Calvelli, who typed drafts of the manuscript.

This book might never have been written if it had not been for the stimulation and help derived from my work with the American Assembly, an activity initiated by General Dwight D. Eisenhower when President of Columbia University. Participation in the preparation of several major Assemblies dealing with the conduct and governance of the corporation, challenged me to make this attempt to achieve greater understanding of its future. Mr. Clifford C. Nelson, President of the American Assembly, disciplined author-editor in his own right, spent many hours in discussions with me and by his penetrating questions clarified some of my thinking. Finally, the availability of an office in the Columbia Graduate School of Business provided the essential means of writing and preparing the manuscript for publication.

COURTNEY C. BROWN
Columbia University
New York City
April, 1979

Introduction

LIKE all major institutions of our society, the business corporation today is the object of many new demands and expectations from society. Because of the power of these demands it is in the midst of a profound, sometimes turbulent transformation over which its managers have limited control. But this transition can be less turbulent for the corporation and its managers, and the results more acceptable to them, if the forces behind it and its goals are sensitively perceived by government officials, the media, labor, investors and the public, as well as by business leaders.

It is of high importance to the nation-at-large that this transition build constructively on the strengths of the business corporation, which, in addition to providing material sustenance and, indeed, abundance, has become a major strength in the preservation of political liberties in our still relatively open society. Without the vitality of the independent business corporation, the functioning of our highly complex industrial nation would be almost completely in the hands of an all-enveloping government. The guidance of the market system would then necessarily be replaced by the compulsions and ineptitudes of centralized administrative rulings. Too much of this has already occurred. And centralized government, while often presenting itself as the protector of the political liberties of citizens, nonetheless frequently feels compelled to subvert the freedom of its citizens. And too much of this has also occurred.

Perhaps the most basic—and positive—aspect of this transformation, as it affects the business corporation, is its shift from an organization conscious of a single purpose (profit) to one conscious of a multiplicity of purposes (economic, social, psychological, educational, environmental, and even political). In recognizing these changes in the corporation, our concern is not so much to condone or condemn these reflections of current societal trends; it is rather to identify and analyze objectively some of the implications—and, indeed, some of the risks—for business and for society as the former adapts to the broadened expectations of the public.

The central issue involved with the current transformation of the business corporation—and the central issue of this book—is not the contest between private enterprise and government for control of the economy, nor the question of the nature and purpose of controls that each might exercise. Rather, this book attempts to root out some of the underlying influences at work on society and business, and bring them to the level of visibility. To do so involves a brief examination of the early societal values that have characterized Western civilization, how these characteristic attitudes have shifted through the centuries, and how their current modifications are affecting the business corporation.

It is one of the observations of this book that when such deep groundswells of conceptual and valuational change were opposed in the past, the resistance in the end often proved useless. History shows that eventually they prove irresistible. Those organizations and institutions that have blindly opposed them have simply disappeared; those that have been more flexible have gradually adjusted to their newly emerging environment and survived. In view of this, there is urgently needed both a modification of public and government attitudes toward business, and a broadened concept of purpose and social service by business. Both are required to assure that the traditional advantages of the private enterprise corporation will survive.

The major shifts in the public's sense of relative values are challenging many of the assumptions that have underpinned the corporation's strength. These shifts are not comfortably contemplated by those conditioned by life careers in business. It is not easy to see how the newly emerging expectations, which carry a strong inflection of egalitarianism, can be successfully reconciled with the values that have made the corporation such a successful contributor to our material well-being. Several of the most conspicuous changes underway seem to involve a fresh commingling of:

Humanism* and compassion	*with*	Science and rationality
Personal security by collective group action	*with*	Self-reliance and individualism
Collaboration to achieve orderly procedures and markets	*with*	Competition and its accompanying rewards and penalties
Decision making by consensus	*with*	The authority of hierarchical structures
Conservation of natural resources	*with*	Aggressive discovery and exploitation

Embedded in these changes are strongly contradictory tendencies. The business corporation first appeared as a significant world influence as science and enlightenment were displacing the earlier preoccupation with religion and the occult. Humanistic concerns had previously dominated a society deprived of material abundance. Civility and collective security were prime considerations. The arrival of science and the scientific method, which found an identifiable

---

* "Humanism" throughout this book is used in the sense of a focused interest on the dignity and worth of the individual and on the egalitarian concern for the disadvantaged. It has neither been used to mean the use of reason as opposed to revelation in understanding human nature, nor to connote an interest in classical letters.

orderliness in nature, turned the intellectual world upside down. Revelation and religious moral philosophy were submerged by scientific objectivity and inquiry. More than the business corporation was born; the ideals of political liberty and individual self-reliance were supported by the notion that harmony with the competitiveness in the world of nature would assure the best quality of human life.

Now there seems to be a resurgence of many of the societal values that dominated Western civilization prior to the age of science and enlightenment. The notions of humanism, group collectivism, collaboration, consensus, and conservation are being reasserted, and they contest the values on which the great successes of the corporation were built. In view of this, there can be no doubt that a major dilemma confronts the leaders of corporations in their effort to adjust to the changing environment. It will take a high order of perception to harmonize the actions of business life with contemporary egalitarian attitudes, and at the same time, retain the efficiency and capability to provide the abundance associated with the postulates of science and rationality.

Some of the impacts on the corporation's governance and structure of these contradictory societal forces are examined here. An effort is made to bring to the surface the principal issues and give greater specification to some of the questions now confronting corporate management. The focus is on the large corporation in its domestic activities, but many of the issues discussed apply, with appropriate changes, to the even more complex world of the multinational corporation. Cultural differences, and confused and changing political policies are added to an already difficult adaptation.

The public debate on the role of the business corporation in contemporary society has reached a crescendo of polemics. Many of the specific issues occupying the public press and even the attention of serious students of the corporation are of peripheral relevance or even irrelevance. Perhaps this examination of some of the underlying forces that society is bringing to bear on the corporation may contribute to a more fruitful search for workable solutions of the dilemma confronting its management.

Increasingly, business judgments are based on purposes that include, but extend beyond, the bottom line. More than the issues normally identified with social responsibility are involved. For example, government regulations, traditionally regarded as good if they contributed to profits and bad if they detracted from profits, must now be further appraised by their impact on the public welfare. While it may be too soon to expect a replacement of the adversary relationship between government and business, in the course of time there may be an opportunity to develop a more constructive identification of their respective functions that would better utilize the strengths of each.

Likewise, attitudes toward the role of competition are now in a transitional phase. Considerations that extend beyond the bottom line must necessarily include a weighing of the costs of restraints to competition in domestic market practices as well as the advantages. Similar considerations must be given to international trade. Personnel practices may become even more considerate and compassionate; labor relations on both sides of the table, more rational. All of these modifications in business practices would come on top of the many changes that have emerged in recent years as business has adjusted to such aspects of social responsibility as conservation, pollution control, the support of the arts, education, and health services.

PART I

The Business Corporation in the Modern World

1

The Business Corporation in Transition

Growing number of doomsayers predict the ultimate demise of the business corporation. With startling frequency, articles appear that question its viability in today's world. Like Rose of Washington Square in the popular song of half a century ago: "She's got no future, but Oh! What a past!!" Such predictions have a certain plausibility, especially if the business corporation is thought of only in terms of the popular criticism that has developed during the past century, and if we neglect the not-so-dramatic and not-so-well-known adaptations that many business corporations have been making, particularly in recent decades, to the changed environment in which they operate. As modifications in the aspirations and attitudes of the public have occurred with dramatic swiftness in the twentieth century, it has been no easy matter to remold the purposes and practices of the business corporation to keep pace—but it has to an extent been done—and it is this remolding that the doomsayers neglect.

3

Change Is Underway

Very significant change in the business corporation is already evident; it has occurred both at home and abroad to adjust the corporation to evolving public attitudes. Thus, for example, changed public attitudes throughout the world have eroded the authoritarianism once associated with corporate executive management. In the United States, this erosion has resulted from expanded government regulation as well as more active and independent monitoring by boards of directors. In Western Europe, the weakening of executive authority is reflected in greater labor participation in decision making, from shop floors to supervisory boards. In East Asia and in much of the lesser-developed world, it has been weakened by demands for direct participation in ownership and control. Everywhere, interest has been shown in greater worker sharing in equity ownership of the corporation. Moreover, public interest and concern about a wide range of perceived impacts of the corporation on the economic, physical, and social environment, as well as various aspects of market behavior, has also worked to reduce business authoritarianism.

The important question then is not whether the business corporation has a future, but rather: What is the probable nature of that future? Can the corporation, in the modified form it is in the process of assuming, be expected to continue to produce the bountiful and ever-increasing abundance that it has provided in years past?

Change in all parts of society is moving at a rapid rate and appears in most places to be irresistible and irreversible. The status quo no longer holds fast, even though the corporation, under the guidelines that have heretofore served it, has delivered extraordinary material benefits during the centuries of its significant existence. The passing of the status quo was

4

recognized nearly two decades ago by Frederick R. Kappel when chairman of the American Telephone & Telegraph Co.:

> We in business are doing more than earning profits. We are doing more than producing goods and services. We are working to help build a political and social system different in important respects from any other. . . .[1]

In the transition, the simplistic purposes and guidelines that the corporation inherited from the past have become blurred. No longer sufficient is the corporate quest only for improved efficiency, competitive success, and maximized profits. New tasks have been assigned by public pressures, tasks for which executive management in many cases is not prepared.

Diminishing Public Approval

The hesitant response of management to demands for change, demonstrating more caution than perceptive enthusiasm, has resulted in growing public disapproval and frequent challenges to the legitimacy of the corporation. The public is confused and skeptical. For its part, corporate management often finds it hard to understand public attitudes. Government, a promoter and staunch supporter of the business corporation in its early days, now usually assumes the posture of an adversary, with public approval.

This adversary relationship is pursued through an elaborately developed crosshatch of regulatory compulsions—some of which are inconsistent with one another—which has shifted many decisions from the corporate manager to government bureaucrats. Business is seen as inconsistent because of its own ambivalent and confused attitudes toward government regulations: some are deemed good, and some bad, depending, it seems, on their short-run effects on profit or on operating freedom. The labyrinth of regulation is a reflection of basic changes in a society that is itself revising

5

its mores and values, and the business response does little to encourage public hopes that business truly understands these changes that are compelling modification in all principal institutions, social, political, educational, artistic, and economic.

The Case for the Single Purpose Corporation

Those who continue to regard the large corporation as a purely profit-making organization, in contrast to a socioeconomic institution of society, would find no inconsistency in these variable attitudes of the businessman toward government regulations. To them, the purpose of the corporation is simply to maximize profits. By making more money, the corporation, they say, performs the full range of its social obligations. If markets are effectively competitive, the corporation will provide the goods and services wanted by the public, will allocate the national resources efficiently, and create growing employment opportunities. Continuous competitive pressure for greater efficiency will assure the public an expanding flow of material goods and services at decreasing real unit costs.

And the corporation, it is held, is ill-suited to accept the newly emerging social responsibilities, which cost money— money that is not available when the competitive situation limits profits to the cost of obtaining capital from investors. In this situation, each factor of production—capital, labor, materials, and technology—earns only its own competitive rewards, and there is no surplus for good deeds. Acceptance of the costs of socially responsible action is, in this view, equivalent to a confession of guilt under the antitrust laws. In a perfectly competitive situation, there would be no surplus. Moreover, corporate managers are believed to be singularly unperceptive about the nonmarketable needs of society.

Why should the alleviation of those needs be turned over to what is held to be, in essence, self-selected private oligarchies?

When the corporation is conceived to have purely a profit-making purpose, a strong case can be made for adhering to traditional guidelines and the existing legal framework for the determination of its policies and practices, harsh and uncompassionate though they may at times be. It is when the business corporation is urged to exercise a major influence beyond its business functions that ambiguity of purpose and practice begins to appear. And many now feel that the corporation cannot escape the expanded social expectations of a people that now enjoys a material abundance that is the result of its own spectacular economic success. The large corporation, they believe, is not the "economic man" of the classical economists now grown up; it is rather the nexus of life in all industrially developed democracies.

The Corporation's "Quasi-Constituencies"

The basic legitimacy of the corporation has been and is grounded on stockholder ownership; stockholders are still the only constituency of a corporation's management that is recognized by corporate law. But a shadow on this legitimacy is now felt by some because of the tenuous control exercised by all but a few stockholders. The process of voting by proxy, in normal circumstances, is far from effective control.

Further, management has, in a substantive sense, acquired additional quasi-constituencies: customers, employees, suppliers, cultural and educational organizations, and environmentalists. The legal recognition of these new quasi-constituencies is found in general legislation—which is in part coercive and in part permissive—not in corporate law. The number of laws related to these quasi-constituencies' concerns is enormous. Thus, laws that constrain the corporation have been passed in the fields of labor and personnel, environment, conservation, and product integrity; other laws such as those granting tax credits for charitable contributions, have facilitated the achievement of socially desirable ends.

Hazards to the Corporation and Society

There are two major hazards involved in the transition of the corporation from a solely profit-making organization to a socioeconomic institution of society. The first is the likely dilution of the sharp-edged compulsions for continuous improvement of efficiency. The inclusion of societal considerations in strategic planning cannot fail to modify the processes of decision making. Careful consideration of administrative structure and procedures is required to preserve, to the maximum extent possible consistent with social performance, the effectiveness of the corporation in its traditional functions. More will be said of this important matter in later chapters.

The second of these hazards involves a risk to society rather than directly to the corporation. Professor Theodore Levitt of Harvard observed several years ago:

> . . . the danger is that all these things . . . will turn the corporation into a twentieth-century equivalent of the medieval church. The corporation would eventually invest itself with all-embracing duties, obligations, and finally powers, ministering to the whole man, and molding him and society in the image of the corporation's narrow ambitions and its essentially unsocial needs.[2]

The truth of the matter is that business management in general feels as uncomfortable about accepting societal functions as Professor Levitt views their possible assumption. There is a realization that, as now motivated and organized, the leadership of the corporation is ill-prepared for such a role. The concern of management is rather to find some identified limits to the socially responsible tasks assigned by public pressures. There is, nevertheless, an awareness that unless business accepts an expanded role, freedom to perform its present functions will be progressively circumscribed by the imposition of governmental regulations. There is an accompanying awareness that a broadening of corporate purposes will require the collective wisdom of personnel with a diversity of interests and experience to share in the development of corporate policy and practice.

Management's Dilemma

A dilemma is a set of circumstances in which the available courses of action are both more or less disagreeable. Corporate management is confronted with a dilemma. It would be pleasant if the rules that guided the corporation to success could be left unmolested and without the penalties of public and governmental encroachment. That is the position often taken publicly by business spokesmen. But experience has demonstrated that efforts to get public acceptance of this position have failed. The argument, cast in terms of free enterprise, that abundance has resulted from the guidelines of the past, simply has not impressed the contemporary public. Government encroachment, loss of public approbation, and the emergence of a defensive state of mind by business have been the end product of these efforts.

The other horn of the dilemma is the problems that stem from the acceptance by corporate management of a broadened range of societal concerns and activities, some of which are closely associated with business affairs and some of which are fairly tangential to business. In accepting this course, some present satisfactions are lost; a clear-cut purpose measured by quantitative results is over-laid by what appears to be a confusion of ill-defined objectives related to quality-of-life considerations. A diversity of new talents and experiences is required in the decision-making process to supplement those conditioned by careers in business. A sharing of authority is involved in either case: a sharing with the government, on the one hand, or with those brought into the orbit of decision making to supplement the purely business experience, on the other.

There is probably no fully satisfactory resolution for executive management of these deep-seated changes that are occurring in the evolution of the corporation. The best that can be hoped for is a reconciliation within the context of the corporation of the societal values of the past with those that have newly emerged.

Public Policy Alternatives

Alternatives are available for the development of future public policy. On the one hand, the past disposition to regard the corporation as a purely profit-driven entity that the public feels must be closely constrained by government can result only in further frustrations. Government regulation of business has already grown to a point where many regard it as excessively costly, ineffective, stifling, and even destructive. The continued insistence by business leaders that the non-economic values of fairness, justice, and equity are secondary to immediate stockholder interests will only assure the further encroachment of regulatory growth.

On the other hand, if corporate leaders prudently move to the acceptance of the premise that the large corporation's activities affect all groups in the community and that their interests must be seriously considered, the decisions will be made with a more perceptive awareness of the social implications involved. That could not fail to diminish the public's support of government regulation. It would serve to help assure the longevity of the private business corporation, and thereby the stockholders' interest. Business protests of gov-

ernment encroachment without this basic adjustment of attitude have not been effective, and are unlikely to be in the
future.

Among the important questions awaiting full resolution
are those concerning the extent to which various social costs
should be brought within corporate accounts, costs heretofore placed on the community, in many cases quite uncon-
sciously. Clean air, pure water, and product safety challenge
efficiency and low unit costs; energy and materials conservation restrain the growth of the GNP and jobs. These are
major issues that involve significant trade-offs. They require
decisions as to whether, and if so how much, the real or
imputed costs should be borne by the corporation—which
means within the market system—or continue to be dis-
tributed to the community at large in taxes, in discomfort,
or perhaps in disappointing material growth.

The achievement of equality of opportunity, a problem
that starts in the community and the educational system, is
now projected, with its attendent costs, into the personnel
practices of the corporation. The costs cannot be wished
away, only shifted. The basic adjustment will be the extent
to which the corporation will become a conduit to transfer
to the marketplace where they can be seen and measured,
those social costs that have heretofore been hidden.

Adaptation is made more difficult by several unchallenged
assumptions deeply embedded in our folklore and in our
corporate law. According to a former dean of the Yale Law
School, Eugene Rostow, "The law books have always said
that the board of directors owes a simple-minded duty of
unswerving loyalty to the stockholders, and only to the
stockholders." Yet executive managers, delegated by the
board of directors to operate the large modern corporation,
have found it necessary and expedient to recognize other constituencies. Long-range company interests, as well as government legislation and regulation, have required it. Other

groups than stockholders now share the attention, if not the loyalty of corporate boards and operating management, and, often in the case of personnel, both the attention and the loyalty.

As Professor Melvin Anshen of the Columbia Business School has said:

> Specific interest groups in our society (environmentalists, minorities, women, consumerists, etc.) are looking at specific aspects of corporate behavior and are saying, "Right here the costs of business practices outweigh the benefits; let's change the rules." No one seems to be considering the total economic implications of the aggregate of all pressures for changed behavior. This is a job for far-sighted business leaders, even business philosophers. There can be no doubt that if the corporation is to continue to generate a rising volume of economic wealth within a market system, while retaining democratic political institutions and personal freedoms, it must keep many of its traditional characteristics. Equally, there can be no doubt that if it is to survive, it must be selective and flexibly adaptive to strong and justified pressures for change.

Dual Influences of the Business Corporation

Part of the molding of public attitudes has resulted from the provision by the business corporation of an unprecedented level of material well-being. With six percent of the population, the United States, where the corporation has had its greatest expansion, currently enjoys some 30 percent of the world's production. It is common knowledge that our use of energy per capita exceeds that of most other industrialized nations.

More and more, people have been brought directly or indirectly into the orbit of the corporation's influence. It is no overstatement to say that the U.S. business corporation is the *major* institution conditioning most aspects of the daily life of every one of us—more so than political institutions, the church, or educational or cultural activities. No data have been compiled, but intuitive judgment supports the view that the man-woman hours spent in serving and thinking about the affairs of the corporation in the aggregate exceed those devoted to any other activity.

Less frequently recognized has been the influence of the corporation on the evolution of political institutions. The world's work is done by the voluntary or compulsory collaboration of groups—family, tribe, voluntary association, or government. Rejecting private business organizations as a desirable expression of voluntary association, some societies have assigned the functions of production and distribution to government. When control over production and distribution is in the hands of government, there can be no market system as we know it. The critical decisions about the types of goods produced as well as their quantity, quality, and price must be made by government officials. The result has necessarily been an authoritarian political structure that operates in a milieu of fixed prices and frozen job assignments, and an economy that may or may not conform to public desires—mostly not. Where technology and large-scale production have advanced together, the corporation has far more preserved than impaired the open market system, despite a crescendo of cries about monopoly. Without the corporation it is not possible for a complex advanced society to maintain an open market that registers public desires. Daniel P. Moynihan has put it well: ". . . the market has a lot more to do with the perpetuation of a democratic and libertarian society than you might think." [3] In an industrially developed society, the corporation makes possible the open market, and keeps it open. An open market, political democracy, and personal and intellectual freedoms have an affinity that is indivisible.

By virtue of its contribution to abundance, of its provision of multiple choices, and of opportunities for self-expression

13

through expanding the range and number of jobs, by utilization of technological advances, by its essential role in the preservation of the market system and of democratic political institutions—by all these things the business corporation has emerged as the fulcrum of a free and independent society. That does not mean that major repairs are not necessary. Quite the contrary. But the transition to new priorities has never been, is not now, and will not be a comfortable one. Nor is it likely that managing the future corporation will provide as much fun for the aggressive, hard-hitting, sometimes combative person who has done so much to build its present strength.

It is important that the corporation be preserved with its capacity for material abundance and its potential for extended public service, but in recent decades the evidence is overwhelming that it has been losing its freedom of action with alarming rapidity. The fact of the matter is that the focus of corporate purpose has necessarily come to rest on the balanced development and longevity of the corporation *per se,* and not on any one constituency, not even stockholders, although stockholders should in the long run benefit when this is more widely recognized. This is a profoundly important, but as yet not fully apprehended, shift of purposes and goals. When fully perceived inside and outside the business community, it should clarify many ambiguities associated with public attitudes toward corporations and the conceptions of business leaders about themselves. Their primary loyalty is properly to the corporation itself, and the corporate interest is best served by a balanced recognition of numerous constituencies. The essential nature of "the corporation in transition" lies in the learning experience occurring daily in corporate practice, and in the catch-up needed in corporate law, to recognize the claims of several constituencies. This constructive change is a basic requirement to the preservation of the corporation in a libertarian society.

Notes

1. Frederick R. Kappel, *Vitality in a Business Enterprise* (New York: McGraw-Hill, 1960), p. 5.

2. Theodore Levitt, quoted in "Business's Stake in Education," *Change* (June-July 1978), pp. 15–16.

3. Daniel P. Moynihan in "The Social Responsibility of Business," *Business and Society in Change* (American Telephone & Telegraph Company, 1975), pp. 19–20.

2

Contrasting Social Values

WESTERN Civilization is now in the midst of a fundamental and historic shift from one complex set of values to another. In our speeded-up world, the old is barely interred before the new is fully upon us. In dozens of matters of human concern, new values strange to the modern mind are finding new adherents. Such a shift of values is, of course, not without precedence, even if the rapidity of change is new. When changes took place in centuries past, they had enormous, if slower, impact. One of these was the emergence several centuries ago of secular, man-centered values over religious, God-centered values. That change extended over the sixteenth, seventeenth, and eighteenth centuries, and became triumphant in the nineteenth and early twentieth centuries.

Large sectors of society were compelled to adapt to these shifts throughout this extended period, with the sacrifice of many established ways of life. Centers of power changed. Princes of the church first gave way to princes of the land, who in turn gave way to princes of industrial, commercial, and financial wealth. Even though the process of social change was slow by our current pace, it was irresistible; the glacial pressures could not be denied. Societal institutions, even the most firmly established, were forced to conform or disappear with the passage of time. The church lost its role as the central interest of daily living, small principalities disappeared as political units, and scholastic and a priori thinking was replaced with skeptical and empirical modes of thought.

Many today sense a new shifting of people's values in the United States, and, indeed, throughout the industrialized West. Values inherited from the age of science and reason, such as efficiency and maximum growth, are no longer accepted without reservation. They are now deemed to be too lacking in solicitude for the public welfare, wanting in compassion for the disadvantaged, and lacking in protection for those exposed to exploitation.

The business corporation became, in the late nineteenth and early twentieth centuries, an organizational form expressing the high value society had come to place on rationality, efficiency, competition, and growth. The once unqualified acceptance of those values is now being challenged by a reaffirmation of the contrasting attitudes and behavioral patterns associated with an earlier humanism. In view of these changes, the business community would do well to give thought to modifying and enlarging the traditional and accepted purposes of the business corporation. Adaptation to a changing environment is an elementary principle of survival. Adaptation of the governance of corporations to facilitate a harmonious response to changing public expectations, and to the prospective circumstances of the future, will require perceptive identification of the influences now molding public attitudes. It will involve structural change within the corporation as well as attitudinal change.

Unfortunately, most analyses of the significant difficulties of business corporations are cast in traditional legal or commercial terms, such as the adequacy of capital or trade

17

practices. But, these fail to shed adequate light on the underlying problems. The public debate, for the most part, has dealt with minor issues of form and procedure rather than penetrating to the substantive issues of purposes and goals. The real values of the business corporation—and they are social and political as well as material—will be restored to credibility in the present climate of opinion only when business spokesmen are able to articulate a set of guiding principles that relate the conduct of business to a wide range of human aspirations, not just to material abundance alone. The impact of business corporations on society has become too profound and widespread to be limited to the latter.

To put the matter succinctly, businessmen must learn to think about, talk about, and operate on a broader platform than is provided by purely economic considerations. There are admitted dangers in doing so. The career of a typical businessman yields limited opportunity to develop perceptive understanding of nonbusiness considerations. Moreover, there is a threat to efficiency and profitability when decisions go, in part, beyond economic matters. But there may be no alternative if the conduct of business is to be preserved without further limitation by external restraints.

Concepts that Shaped the Corporation

A brief review of the history of the concepts that characterized the evolution of the modern business corporation is an interesting intellectual exercise. It can help us to understand some of the now troublesome issues that appear to be so intractable—especially the questions of why the public holds the business corporation in such relatively low esteem and why government increasingly appears in the role of adversary rather than its sponsor, or even its friend.

These concepts have their origin respectively in the Middle Ages, the Renaissance, and the Reformation, in the rise of the nation-state and mercantilism, and most particularly in the seventeenth and eighteenth century age of science and reason. At the same time, these early periods also yielded some of the more humanistic attitudes that are now being revived to support criticism of what is perceived by the corporation's detractors to be too narrowly focused commercial purposes.

Orderliness and a passion for certainty, so important for effective corporate management, were sanctified in the Middle Ages. Obedience and correct belief in the authoritative doctrine of an organization, then the medieval church, was accepted as a cardinal virtue. Wealth for its own sake was disapproved, but could be justified as stewardship—somewhat the same image and posture claimed for the professional manager who controls wealth today.

On the other hand, other values and goals of the medieval period are less consistent with the activities of the modern corporation. For example, charitable service to mankind for its own sake finds limited enthusiasm in the modern business corporation. Nor is there a burning compassion for the disadvantaged, and certainly there is no reverence for nature as an awesome and wonderful gift of God, the use of which should be carefully limited. The medieval church's disapproval of paying interest would impose an impossible burden on modern corporate finance.

An inversion of social values began with the Renaissance, which awakened the specious lethargy of the Middle Ages. Medieval rejection of personal pride and the accumulation of wealth shifted into an acceptance of thrift and productive labor as commendable means of individual development. The Reformation went a step further. It released the emerging middle class from the bondage of the church to support the growth of strong monarchies, whose principal function was to assure prosperity for the then newly formed national states. Puritanism, a derivative of the Reformation, elevated

19

the purposes and aims of business society by exalting personal responsibility, discipline, punctuality, honesty, and commitment. Calvin, one of the fathers of puritanism, preached that the paying of interest was not a sin.

The newly established monarchies promoted business with enthusiasm within the limits of their understanding of what was needed. Mercantilism was the result. The corporation emerged as a favored vehicle to achieve the power, expansion, and national prosperity that Machiavelli had named as constituting the art of government. It had certain advantages such as limited liability, the ability to consolidate capital, and centralized administration. Governments granted to corporations monopolistic favors and bounty, especially in the newly discovered parts of the world. National prosperity was sought by helping private, joint stock companies to succeed. Governments took over from the medieval guilds the regulation of market sharing, prices, and product quality. National prosperity, as viewed by the theorists of mercantilism, was primarily concerned with the notion of increasing the nation's wealth by developing a favorable balance of trade—an excess of exports over imports—in order to accumulate ever larger stocks of gold and silver. (The modern concept of macroeconomics, namely the stimulation and control of total economic activity through the manipulation of aggregate demand by national monetary and fiscal policies, was then unknown, of course.)

The influence on business of the emergence of intellectual interest in the natural sciences would be hard to exaggerate. As the seventeenth century turned into the eighteenth, the preoccupation with natural science made two major contributions to public attitudes, despite the disdain held for the new methods of science by the traditional and still reigning humanists. Allying mathematics and experimental observation, Isaac Newton and his successors found an orderliness in nature, the processes of which could be adapted to man's use. Nature was no longer something to be revered and used sparingly. Rather, it was a bountiful treasure to be exploited.

The idea of an all-embracing natural order led to the second major contribution. Since nature was found to be orderly, instead of seeking reasons for, or attributing occult purposes to, nature, the direction of thought was to let every man be free to model himself after the natural. Nature and the natural became the ideal, and what was natural was reasonable.

The effect on political structures and social science was profound. Absolute monarchies and the elaborate controls of mercantilism became irksome, even though they had been supported by the rising commercial interests. If natural science prescribed freedom for the activities of man in his relation to nature, should not the same hold true in his relations to his fellow men? To limit the power of the monarch, the ancient concept of a social contract was revived from Roman law and from the mutual obligation feudal lords had had with their serfs. Ultimate power, it was held, rests with the people. Those powers and rights not specifically delegated remain with the people, a basic principle of political federalism. The writings of John Locke opened a path toward constitutional monarchy and away from political absolutism. The self-reliance inherited from the Reformation, and given further expression in puritanism, displaced collectivism and implanted individualism as a social ideal.

In economic science, then called political economy, revision of thought also occurred. Adam Smith, in 1776, corrected several of the false assumptions that had characterized mercantilism. The wealth of a nation, he held, is in its productive capability, not in its store of gold and other precious metals. Domestic trade and commerce, as well as manufacturing and agricultural production, added to economic value. Business, unlike politics, was not what is now called a zero-sum game, where one's gain is another's loss. Both

21

parties to a transaction could gain. Price, if left alone, would adjust to a point that would clear markets. Price controls, whether based on tradition, an idea of fairness, or other criteria, would simply get in the way.

Let government simply set the broad rules of the game that would protect property and contract, Smith held. Let each seek his or her enlightened self-interest in a competitive world, and the "invisible hand" of nature would maximize benefits to society at large. Competition was beginning to be perceived as a basic law of nature. As Charles Darwin later observed, those that were adapted better to the environment would survive, the rest would die out. Competition to survive may be cruel, but many seeing it as a law of nature prescribed it for the development of strength and survival in human society. Success went to those corporations that were the most efficient in the open market.

Centuries of Explosive Growth

Thus, by the middle and end of the eighteenth century, in three major areas of intellectual interest—natural science, political science, and economic science—the broad sweep of thought headed the Western World in the direction of an open society. The corporation had had its adolescence under the tight controls of mercantilism. It had not merely been encouraged, it had been supported by government. The favor was reciprocated by corporate support of the newly emerged national states. Under the libertarianism of the late eighteenth century, the corporation flowered. In the early nineteenth century, it achieved the status of a "legal person." It matured in the industrial environment of the late nineteenth century. The idea of an expanded growth of material wealth, which played no part in intellectual life until the arrival of the age of science, began to take its place alongside the newly identified laws of nature and the ancient religious traditions in its influence on mankind.

The eighteenth century was truly an auspicious time for the Western World. With the onrush of science and technology, with government commitment to facilitate national prosperity, and with the acceptance of nature as something to be exploited rather than revered, the stage was set for an explosive growth of material production. And the business corporation was the prime vehicle. It reconciled the widely held ideal of private property, the reality of industrial concentration mandated by technology, and the economic advantages of large size. As a part of the same world, it was inevitable that the managers of the business corporation should conceive of its functions as harmonizing with the laws of natural science and the orderly values they suggested.

Origins of the Current Dilemma

When Leonardo da Vinci, an early scientist as well as a great artist, observed that "Whoever appeals to authority applies not his intellect but his memory," [1] he disdained the authority of the church and the ancient moral philosophers. He was not referring to the laws of natural science, the discovery of which was even then challenging the best minds of the day. Objective inquiry and rigorous analytical procedures became the rational means to seek truth. Successive discoveries required flexible adjustment of thought to new facts and circumstances, especially in the field of technology.

Two major consequences ensued for the business corporation. The opportunity that was associated with its development attracted men of intelligence, imagination, courage, and action to its leadership; and the ability to adapt the corporation without excessive restraint became a matter of increasing importance. External political regulation became

23

onerous. The invocation of natural liberty was used to support, and still supports, the corporation's challenge to external political restraints.

The desire of corporate business leaders to function without external hindrance, however, stood in marked contrast to their expectation of conformity from associates within the organization. Individual performance came to be judged by results that were consistent with decreed purposes. Good intentions were of less relevance than they had been in the religious era. Compassion is seldom an enduring sentiment, and it became less and less significant as the goals of low cost and efficiency emerged to support continuous growth, an idea now dominant for so long it has become a corporate gospel.

Effective use of the resources marshalled under the corporate form has been the principal generator of success in creating additional material wealth, in providing more jobs and, indeed, in acquiring still more capital. But the means of achieving efficiency, that is, low unit costs, tend to make solicitude difficult and, in some situations, competitively prohibitive. This does not mean that there is a one-for-one trade-off. In some situations, short-term expenditures may result in a long-term profit improvement, as for example with employee medical benefits. But unfortunately management careers are now typically evaluated by reference to the bottom line over short periods of time.

The humane and social tasks that the public now expects of business corporations generally make a poor fit with the traditional activities and purposes in which corporations so spectacularly succeeded. Yet despite, or perhaps because of, two hundred years of enormous material success, there is now insistent questioning whether an economic system should be judged alone by the abundance it creates. There is interest in how that system exerts its influence—for better or worse—on the human personality. And so once again the institutions rooted in the attitudes and methods of natural science, just as when they first appeared, are confronted by those whose primary commitment is to the universal concern for the "whole man," not simply "economic man." The business corporation is one of the principal organizations so confronted. And that, in essence, is the source of the corporate dilemma.

The Shifting Role of Government

The rearrangement long ago of religious and secular values also found its reflection in the objects of public veneration. The attribution of divine guidance, which had given absolute authority to the princes of the medieval church, was transmuted, for the kings of the newly emerging nations, into the divine right to rule. A public enthusiasm that translated into impassioned and patriotic allegiance to the quickly developing nation-states had the characteristics of religious commitment; and the king was the personification of the nation. To a significant degree, the nation replaced the church as the central object of devotion. The nation, initially supported in part to encourage and protect the rapidly expanding creators of wealth, in turn shed a part of its acquired respect on the businessman. As viewed by Harold R. Isaacs of Yale, it is

> quite possible, even reasonable, to interpret the whole process as one of identifying the interest of God with those of the creators of the new capitalist system. . . .[2]

The Calvinists believed that the accumulation of capital was a fulfillment of God's work.

The reversal of governmental attitudes toward business since the eighteenth century has been gradual, but persistent. As the ideas of the social contract and the people as the ultimate locus of power eroded the divine right of kings and led toward the formation of constitutions, government was increasingly regarded as the representative and protector of the people. For many years the regulatory authority of the government has struggled with the supporters of economic competition for the latter role. Both have presented themselves as the protector of the public against exploitation by business, but competition has steadily lost ground to government control over the past century.

A shift has occurred, gradual but insistent, from government as supporter and promoter of business to government as a restraint on, and an adversary of, business, a role now widely assumed to be necessary to protect the public. The consumer movement has been built on the premise that business will always take advantage of the public when possible. The enthusiasm for this role of protector by many elected and appointed government officials has led one observer to the view that government is now used as a kind of secular church to make business good and virtuous. Slowness by business management to understand perceptively the changing convictions and expectations of the public, and to incorporate public attitudes into the program and practices of business, has simply led to additional arguments for governmentally imposed regulatory action.

Expanding Business Involvement

A recitation of various newly identified activities expressing social responsibility is the usual means of illustrating the additional directions that public expectations now prescribe for business. This is useful of course, but an alleviation of the business corporation's public disfavor will require a still larger agenda. Product integrity and "good citizenship" are a must, but they are not enough. It will require an attitudinal change that puts societal purposes and goals on a comparable footing with economic aims. That is not an easy shift to make, given the traditions of corporate development and the career training of most corporate executives. Pollution control and environmental protection, conservation, agreeable and safe work conditions, nondiscrimination, employment training, adequate and secure pensions, support of not-for-profit organizations—all are very much alive in public discussions and are part of the social responsibility package. Adaptation of corporate policy and practice to these now generally accepted purposes has been in process for some years, in part self-imposed, in part government-imposed, and all supported by public demand. There is much yet to be done, but progress has been made.

It must be said, however, that the adjustment of business thinking to deal with these now recognized socially responsible activities has not been a comfortable one. The introduction of social performance into business organizations is a genuine innovation. Part of executive management's difficulty in responding is that there is no organized market to register public desires and needs. Emerging societal demands are expressed through the political processes of the nation rather than through the movement of relative prices in the marketplace. The changing social and political influences are unlikely to be sensitively perceived by the business executive with lead time adequate to avoid public condemnation. Failure to have moved more rapidly in concert as a business community in pollution control is a classic example. The real failure was in not initiating a request for legislation, in the formulation and support of which business should have had a leadership role.

Exployment and the Work Cycle

But the currently expanded range of business concerns is destined to expand still further. Extraordinarily complex problems loom ahead that cannot fail to fall within the orbit of corporate interests, problems extending beyond the issues now typically listed under the rubric of *social responsibility*. Some of these will involve a clarification and amplification, it is to be hoped a rectification, of business-government relationships.[3] Others will require a clarification of the appropriate uses of competition and collaboration. But perhaps the most difficult adjustments will require an adaptation to population trends and people's attitudes toward work, in combination with changing rates of economic growth. In recent years there has been a diminution in the rate of total population increase in the United States, but concomitantly there has occurred a remarkable increase in the size of the labor force. In 1950 the figure stood at 63.8 million; in 1977 it was 99.5 million.

And during the same period, the composition of the work force has changed. A quarter century ago, one third of all women of working age were employed; now the figure is above one half. On the other hand, the number of men between ages 25 and 55 in the work force has declined from 97 percent to 94 percent in the past decade.[4] Those born in the postwar baby-boom have now reached working age. They have doubled the number in the labor force under the age of 25. Thus while the labor force as a percentage of the total population has grown remarkably, major modifications have occurred in its composition, and the number of the unemployed as a percentage of the total labor force has proved to be a difficult figure to reduce.

Apart from the bulge of postwar babies, the population is now aging, there being both lower birthrates and deaths at older ages. Births declined from 4,200,000 in 1960 to 2,800,000 in 1976. This declining trend will result in a significant drop in the number of future entrants into the work force. The effect this will have on the working career, on product quality, and on productivity is uncertain. In the absence of a higher rate of future economic growth than now seems in prospect, and with fewer entering and fewer leaving the labor force, it does imply less upward mobility in personal careers, and, therefore, discontent for the more ambitious.

Business, as the nation's principal employer, cannot escape the resentment associated with *unemployment*. Comprehensive data on *underemployment* are not available, but the frustration from less work than desired, or the absence of opportunities to make full use of one's abilities, could become widespread. Some of these tensions may be relieved by a growing number of "dropouts," whose interest in work is diminished. The current reduced birthrate will also help to alleviate the problem by supplying fewer new entrants to the labor market.

A more rapid rate of economic growth would also contribute to an alleviation of these difficulties, but many question whether future rates will equal those of the past. Diminishing supplies and higher real costs of raw materials, particularly sources of energy, imply a slower rate of growth. Minerals output and the production of grains, livestock, fish, and forest products are not keeping pace with world population growth. Conservation and recycling will necessarily become matters of increasing importance. The accumulation of new capital is deemed to be inadequate. In some consumer product markets, there may be incipient signs of satiation— wearing apparel, steel, and interstate highways for example. Nonmaterial desires appear to be working changes in the psychology of material needs as the population becomes more affluent. All of these influences may retard the future rate of economic growth.

The postwar baby-boom that has now reached maturity is itself beginning to influence economic growth. The attitudes among this younger generation are not reliable guides as to how they may feel in later years, but as personal security arrangements have increased, saving or acquisition now seem to have less interest for them. Self-reliance has been, in part, submerged into a search for personal security through collective group action. The rich are often disdained, and zeal for the disadvantaged and concern for humanity tend to exceed personal interest in achievement. After basic needs are met, leisure is often prized above work. A sense of commitment to a job in a business corporation is limited. Some of these characteristics are not unlike the attitudes that go far back into the humanism of the Middle Ages. They are the antithesis of the attitudes of the age of science—or somewhat earlier—of the puritans following the Reformation.

A further perspective is thrown on contemporary attitudes by scholars in the field of psychology. The characterization is made that it was the "public man" who epitomized the ancient world, the "religious man" who dominated the medieval period, the "creative man" who typified the Renaissance, and the "economic man" who moved to center stage in the age of industrialization. Our day, it is observed, has produced the "psychological man"; an inner directed person deeply aware of himself and seeking fulfillment that may not be immediately related to income or status.

And there is some evidence, tentative to be sure, that the consumption or fulfillment ethic has replaced the puritan ethic, that the idea of thrift and sacrifice has lost some of its potency, and that personal security is sought more through collective group action or governmental action than through self-reliance. These radical changes in demography and in attitudes toward work and personal values have begun to induce innovative changes in the personnel practices of corporations. Experiments have been initiated with more flexible working hours ("flexi-time"), and job sharing in which two workers share one job and one set of benefits. Flexibility of selection among fringe benefits is being tried.

The question of appropriate retirement policy is anything but clear in public thinking. Will the normal retirement age continue its voluntary decline as it has in the recent past? In 1957, 38 percent of the over-sixty-five were working. Two decades later the number had dropped to 20 percent. Should mandatory retirement be made illegal before age seventy, as recently enacted by the Congress with certain exceptions, or ageless, as now proposed? Later retirement would relieve discontent among a growing population of elders, especially if accompanied by a gradual reduction of working hours. It would also limit the opportunities for oncoming generations and probably would drain some of the vitality and adjustability from the operations of business. That could impair the ability to adapt to changing circumstances.

There is a troublesome paradox lurking in these personnel concerns of business. Work is still regarded by most as a means of self-expression and personal fulfillment. Yet the opportunity to work with upward mobility may diminish for an increasing segment of the population at the same time as quality-of-life considerations take higher priority in public attention. These problems will be exacerbated as the "bubble" of postwar babies moves through the population age scales. Those of prime working age, 25 to 44, totaled 39 million in 1975; by 1990 they will total 60.5 million.

It is anything but clear how the values of justice, compassion, and mutual service might affect a situation of chronic underutilization of abilities or of underemployment, should such a condition materialize. Moreover, the growing number of retirees and other inactive people will have to be supported nationally by a contracting number of newly arrived workers with inevitable strains on pension and social security arrangements. Numerous programs have been developed by both the government and by business corporations. In addition to the national Social Security program, the employee benefit plans include: workers' compensation, unemployment insurance, private retirement systems, group life and medical insurance plans, sickness benefits, and others. Some, nonetheless, fear that inadequate financial preparation is being made to meet the steadily rising costs of tomorrow. Of even greater concern, these future commitments to a non-working population may be developing into a burden that will be resented by the working population in the years to come.

Only one thing seems clear: the business corporation will be profoundly affected. The values and commitments of a libertarian society, and the values and commitments that so successfully permitted the corporation to take advantage of the discoveries in natural science for more than two centuries, can be preserved only if ways can be found to supplement the corporation's traditional aims without excessive impairment of the values on which its success has been built. The values of humanism need a fresh reconciliation with those that are inspired by the natural sciences; and that is a fusion that has been difficult to accomplish.

But the corporation is adapting. Significant—even though reluctant—change has occurred. Some social costs previously borne by the public at large have been shifted to the corporation's accounts. Real unit costs of producing goods and services have risen, contrary to the results expected from progress in technology and competition in efficiency. Among other things, incremental costs of job training, the provision of personal security, and the ballooning costs of record-keeping associated with growing regulatory procedures have added significantly to real unit costs.

There is no prospect that these tendencies will be reversed; rather, they will be accentuated as new problems appear in the years ahead. Adaptation and flexibility will be required as cardinal virtues of business leadership. Businessmen must imaginatively appraise the future and rely less on the past. They must understand social needs as well as business concerns. They would be wise to remember Leonardo da Vinci's words that were quoted earlier and that were so helpful when the early corporation was adjusting to the new disciplines of natural science: "Whoever appeals to authority applies not his intellect but his memory." Then it was the natural scientists encroaching on the religious humanists. Now it is almost the reverse; secular humanists encroaching on the natural scientists.

Some of the business adjustments will be of an organizational nature; others will demand a shift of resources to other activities—manufacturing to service, for example; or the development of joint ventures with governmental agencies; or the extension of operations to a global basis, where there may be different, but no less intractable, problems. The most difficult adjustments, however, will be those that make *routine* the practice of placing societal considerations alongside the economic at all stages. It will be no easy task to achieve an optimum blend of the two.

A departure from the overriding objective of maximizing profits in short periods can be rationalized only by a conviction that socially desirable action best assures maximum benefits and a minimum of penalties in the long run. Who shall decide? Should all in the organization be encouraged to make a balanced appraisal? Should the process of decision making be deliberately designed to assure inputs of alternative points of view resulting in what some have called the "creative tensions" of adversary relationships? This, of course, would involve a fundamental modification in the traditional patterns of business behavior, which now emphasize authoritative acceptance of a single voice. These adjustments will require imaginative leadership and, above all, flexibility and adaptability in the corporate structure and personnel.

Before examining some of the changes in the patterns of corporate decision making and the structural modifications required by an enlargement of corporate purposes, a review in the next chapter of several issues that occupy popular attention may convince us that the basic difficulties have not been seriously addressed in public debate.

Notes

1. Leonardo da Vinci, cited in John Herman Randall, Jr., *The Making of the Modern Mind: A Survey of the Intellectual Background of the Present Age,* revised edition (Cambridge, Mass.: Houghton Mifflin Company, 1940), p. 220.

2. Harold R. Isaacs, *Foreign Affairs,* April 1975, p. 440.

3. Something will be said of this in the penultimate chapter of this book.

4. *Business Week,* November 14, 1977, p. 156.

PART II

The Issues: Apparent and Real

3

Apparent Issues

Despite an awareness of the pressures to expand their service to society, the managers of business corporations have displayed an understandable reluctance to move quickly. When a public commitment is made to serve their numerous quasi-constituencies, a company's managers are placed in the exposed position of having to judge among the claims of several contending groups. The result has been a crescendo of cries against business from many points of the public compass. Criticism has especially been directed at the "deliberate haste" that has characterized the structural adjustments and the development of new policies and practices by business.

The public attack has not been directed with conspicuous understanding of business realities, nor has the business response been distinguished. The former has endorsed an elaboration of governmental controls rather than first exploring opportunities for change within the business corporation. Since, of course, the dissatisfied public has little competence for exploring the possibilities for change within the business corporation, it tends to turn to government for relief. Management for its part has taken some voluntary initiatives, but apparently not enough to satisfy the public.

It has also launched a massive public relations program of so-called economic education, the substance of which is only partially convincing at best.

The attack on business is currently clustered around several main issues: an extension of controls through federal chartering, or a minimum standards act, efforts to obtain constituency representation on boards of directors, the old chestnut of interlocking directors, and greater stockholder participation, or what has come to be called stockholder democracy. And then there is the long-continued and long-confused effort to control behavior in the open market through the antitrust laws. The role of business in inflation, unemployment, product quality, and so-called questionable payments abroad are also part of the catalogue of criticism. Few of these issues give promise of hitting the target of required change; few will equip business for the new dual role of simultaneously providing material abundance and more humane life experiences; nor is the defensive program of economic education by business addressed to these dual objectives. We will argue that the time and effort assigned to some of these issues are more than is required to serve the public interest; others, such as inflation and competitive behavior, deserve more attention from everyone.

The Content of Economic Education

It is widely believed that business is essentially exploitative, that if left alone it will serve only itself, and that economic competition has been so greatly weakened that it can no longer be relied upon to protect the public. Gone is the conviction that actions to serve enlightened self-interest in a competitive situation will result in the greatest good for the greatest number. Profits are thought to be excessive and to represent a withdrawal from the stream of national income at the expense of those who need a larger piece of the economic pie. These beliefs are consistent with the current commitment to egalitarianism.

Large sums and much executive time and talent have been expended by business to persuade "the public" of the business position and to discredit critics, all with few discernable results. Unfortunately, the effort on balance may have been counter-productive in that it has placed business in a defensive posture, seeking, in the opinion of far too many, to protect privileged and entrenched positions. The "public" to be reached has been identified as including employees, elementary and secondary school teachers, occasionally members of college faculties, and a cross section of the populace. Better understanding of the economic system and the nature of business operations, it has been held, will moderate public criticism and reduce the pressures for continuous expansion of governmental regulations and control. The content of the educational effort is elementary, designed to achieve as much popular attention as is possible using "the dismal science of economics." To carry out this effort, the number of public relations functionaries has been expanded significantly.

Part of the confusion associated with this program in the public mind may be that the program materials are overly defensive, answering the charges of monopoly and excessive profits in the terms in which they are made.

Business also has a common practice of emphasizing in its public releases a percentage change of net profits from a previous period, reported as a residual "bottom line," rather than focusing attention of the rate of return on invested capital. A 25 to 50 percent increase over the year before is often confused as an exorbitant return, thus confirming the public's impression of monopolistic practices.

What needs to be conveyed to the public, in a program of economic education, about monopoly and competition is quite a different matter. Two tests are frequently used by economists to measure the alleged decline of competition;

the growing size of firms and the share of an ambiguously defined market held by one or several firms. But the return earned on invested capital is a more reliable measure. As some scholars have found after careful research in which the rate of return is adjusted for inflation, there has been no significant overall impairment of the ability of competition to protect the consumer. Quite the contrary, rates of return so adjusted have declined alarmingly in recent decades, thus threatening the adequacy of capital formation. But the government's case for expanding regulatory activity rests in large measure on the failure of economic competition to do its work, or on the inability of the public to identify and reject products and services that lack integrity. Both of these are dubious assumptions.

The operation of a workably competitive economy surrounds business with constraints that are ever present in the thinking of business management. The possibility of new competitors entering the market can never be disregarded. The broadened range and shortened time spans of mass communications assures greater public knowledge of the degree of integrity and kind of performance of a wide variety of goods and services. Customer loyalties can and have shifted rapidly. The opportunity for alternate choices has broadened—not contracted.

Moreover, the verity that profits, regardless of their level, have work to do in the service of the public seems to have been lost in the debate on whether they are too high or too low. The point of regulatory reference is measured against some inherent notion of fairness rather than the public's desire or lack of desire for more or less production among a wide variety of goods and services. The energy program of the nation is currently suffering and losing valuable time from this confusion. When there is a pressing public need or desire for more of a product or service, profits should increase to attract additional capital to induce an increase of supply. When the public need or desire for an economic good or service is diminishing, profits should contract to induce a removal of capital from the activity; more dog collars, fewer horse collars, for example.

The mobility of capital among different types of production is of concurrent importance with the aggregate formation of capital if the business community is to serve the public interest effectively. The intervention of government has demonstrated limited awareness of this fact. Unfortunately, the business response to its critics regarding profits has frequently been in terms of the *fairness* of profits rather than of their *function*. Profits as an economic function are good for the public, not bad, yet business spokesmen have at times felt so defensive that they have avoided mention of the term altogether.

Business is right in resisting the many governmental encroachments on pricing in free and open markets, whether they be capital markets, commodity markets, product markets, or service markets. Relative prices, just as profits, have work to do. They register changes in public needs and desires, and thus serve as guides in the allocation of productive resources, including human effort. Unfortunately, business leaders seem more aware of the debilitating results of governmental interference with price behavior than of their own interference with price movement in the free market. Interference with the free adjustment of prices, whether by government or business, limits the terms on which a libertarian and open society can exist. A case, of course, can be made for such interference in a variety of specific situations, but the burden of proof for intervention should be on government and on business in each instance, especially as regards restraints on new entry into the market.

There is a difference between protecting and preserving

competition, and protecting and preserving competitors. Both business and government, particularly the latter, have been guilty of confusing the two. Protection of competition is in harmony with what were taken to be the laws of nature on which the corporation built its spectacular successes. Protection of competitors through intervention in the movement of prices in free markets is the antithesis of the principle of survival of the fittest. Paul Weaver was perceptive when he noted in his June 1977 *Fortune* article the businessman's opinion that "government intervention in the marketplace is not just a lapse from principle, but an irrational attempt to repeal the laws of nature." [1]

But business itself cannot claim title to purism as libertarian free enterprisers. The endorsement by business of direct or indirect subsidies, or of regulatory procedures that protect competitors, diminishes competition. Could this be the result of too great a readiness to qualify the principles on which the corporation has prospered, or could it be that the implications are not fully apprehended? Is economic regulation acceptable, but social regulation never? Intervention is not a matter of absolute right or wrong; its rightness or wrongness depends on the circumstances. But its significance should be understood. As Weaver continues in his *Fortune* article: "The only job of economic education facing American businessmen is the one they have to do on themselves by themselves." [2]

The opportunity for self-adjustment and for self-regulation can be best preserved in a libertarian political climate. That condition is more likely to be available if the business community fully understands the requirements and meaning of *libertarianism*. It is quite different from the modern so-called *liberalism*, which has largely come to mean financial outlays to alleviate public distress and political pressures, accompanied by various types of controls. It may be that the business community is the only one that can effectively serve as the custodian of a libertarian and open society. The political world has become excessively committed to free-spending *liberalism,* which is the antithesis of classical liberalism as it was known when the restraints of mercantilism were being shed by the Philosophical Radicals.

Business leadership can qualify for the exalted role of custodian of libertarianism only if it understands the damage that is done the open society by its own pleas for political and financial relief when the competitive situation becomes difficult. There are penalties as well as rewards in the free economy. As Carl A. Gerstacher of Dow Chemical said recently, "When things get so bad we welcome government controls, we perform an act somewhat akin to Cleopatra's clasping the viper to her bosom." [3]

The adversary posture of government toward business unfortunately now has deep roots. If the voice of business is to be heard better and earn credibility in government and media circles as well as in the halls of academe, it must demonstrate convincingly, in free and open markets, that competition is still effective in the role of public protector. And, business by action and word must convey an awareness of the societal as well as the material services it has provided and has the opportunity to provide on a broadening scale to the public. Conversely, it is a mistake for business to adopt the posture of being the custodian of economic sophistication with a desire to share that knowledge with the public.

More importantly, business must articulate more clearly its opportunities and its commitment to respond to the public's aspirations. Those usually identified as intellectuals engaged in the mass media and in academe, to quote the late Lionel Trilling,

> . . . take virtually for granted the adversary intention, the actual subversive intention . . . of detaching the reader

from habits of thought and feeling that the larger culture imposes, of giving him a ground and vantage point from which to judge and condemn. . . .[4]

This may also be said of many government officials, some of whom have reached their present assignments by way of the press or the campus. The intelligentsia's behavior is more determined by their personal character than by the nature of the field of work with which they are associated. Witness the often-strained relationships between those who speak for government and those who tear government officers apart in the mass media.

There is little, if anything, that business can say to ameliorate the adversary attitudes of many government officials. But if this condition can be improved through rapprochement or otherwise, it will be the result of informed and enlightened practice by business rather than by large expenditures to "educate" the public about business. It may not be possible fully to recapture the old relationship of government as sponsor of business—many would say it is not even desirable —but the public good would be served by limiting the enthusiasm for opposition by governmental officers. Even the intelligentsia, despite a predisposition to find their enemies on the right—never on the left—may begin to discover some of the essential values of the business world.

Quasi-Constituency Representation and Interlocking Boards

Traditionally, it has been held that a good member of a board of directors would always place the interest of the corporation above that of any particular constituency, irrespective of past or present associations. This has been an overriding guideline in corporate governance. But now another of the issues that have captured more public attention than they deserve challenges this stance and holds that, since the activities of the corporation affect different groups differently, each group should have representation on its governing board who will look out for the interests of that group. This challenge confronts us with a subtle, if not profound, issue.

The legal foundation of the corporation, it has frequently been said in public statements by corporate executives, rests on the fact that the board represents stockholders as its constituency—and, in the legal sense, only the stockholders. In practice, however, the leadership of the corporation has come in recent decades to recognize numerous other constituencies, or "quasi-constituencies," because doing so *was in the long-term interest of stockholders*. Frank W. Abrams of Standard Oil (N.J.), now Exxon, saw more than a quarter of a century ago that a job of management is to maintain "an equitable and working balance among the claims of the various directly interested groups."

Thus, if stockholders are now represented at the board, one might plausibly ask, why would it not be logical to recognize these quasi-constituencies, with their advocates participating in board discussions and decisions, assuming that representatives of consumers, labor, environmental groups, etc., were of the same level of competence in their interests as were other members of the board. The question is raised not so much to resolve the issue here, but to emphasize the subtleties encountered in the question of constituency representation on the board and the degree to which it might on occasion be exercised.

Another aspect of constituency representation that is seldom recognized is its relation to the issue of interlocking directors. Corporations are sellers to, and buyers from, other corporations. Should those who serve on the boards of these buyer or seller corporations be excluded from a company's board? Outside counsel, and investment and commercial bankers are sellers of services to the corporation, just as suppliers of raw materials and product components are sellers. Indeed, the corporation's activities embrace continuous and comprehensive buying and selling. It would be hard to identify a perceptive, qualified board member who was not involved in some way in a major corporation's market activities, the degree being a matter of proximity, of continuity, and of longevity. In these relationships, when does a conflict of affiliated interests constitute a meaningful conflict?

The significance, or lack thereof, of many continuing buyer-seller relationships has been enhanced by the market behavior now characteristic of the large corporation. Dr. Arthur M. Okun put it well in a talk to the Economic Club of Chicago in October of 1977:

> . . . the nature of price and wage making has been transformed in the modern era. We live in a world dominated by cost-oriented prices and equity-oriented wages.
>
> The pricing policies designed to treat customers reasonably and maintain their loyalty in good times and bad times rely heavily on making up some standard measure of costs.
>
> Similarly, the long-term interests of skilled workers and employers in maintaining their relationships is the key to wage decisions in both union and nonunion situations.
>
> Employers have investments in a trained, reliable, and loyal work force. Workers seek and generally obtain equitable treatments, and the basic test of equity is that their pay is raised in line with the pay increases of other workers in similar situations—creating a pattern of wages following wages.
>
> The customer and career relationships are not creations of evil monopolies but rather adaptations to a complex interdependent economy in which customers and suppliers, workers and employers benefit greatly from continuing relationships.[5]

This sounds not unlike the buyer-seller relationships that have long existed among corporations, and between corporations and their bankers and their legal counsels.

Interlocking directors of different corporations are sometimes thought to be prohibited when the corporations are significant buyers and sellers to each other; also when they are significant competing sellers in what are believed to be similar markets, such as steel and aluminum, vinyl and painted wall covering, etc. But it is not, a priori, the case that genuine conflicts of interests exist in such instances. They may or may not, depending on the extent of the influence that individual board members have on company practice, and this can only be determined by a careful empirical examination of the facts in each case.

The regulatory action taken in recent cases suggests, however, as much a punitive motivation as a real concern to protect the public. No one can be sure that the alleged conflicts of interests of many interlocking directors differs from or is equal to comparable conflicts that exist in other affairs throughout society. And even though a director may wish to pursue a special interest at the expense of the corporation on whose board he or she serves, or at the expense of the public, his or her ability to do so is, in fact, often quite limited.

The interlocking director issue at the present seems to be one created more by the law and the fear of financial control of several generations ago than by present substance. Its major current significance is that it is an encouragement of "cronyism," which weakens the board's independence, not that it implies "an overwhelming potential for antitrust abuse and possible conflicts of interest" as has been reported by the staff of a U.S. Senate subcommittee. That conclusion reflects the attitudes that existed at the turn of the century, when interlocking boards were believed to be the means of exercising financial controls across a broad spectrum of corporate activities.

A more effective kind of control is now available to the administrators of large accumulations of shares in pension funds, trust accounts, and mutual investment trusts. So far, however, these administrators have chosen to express their views by buying or selling their shares rather than by seeking direct control through the election of directors—with one exception. Managers of labor union pension funds have used the large accumulations in the pension funds of certain companies' securities to force the resignation of several corporate board members of companies that have resisted union organizing drives.

Another situation that complicates the issue of quasi-constituency representation exists when the traditions—or lethargy—of an existing board makes long overdue change difficult—if not impossible—to achieve. When General Motors added the Reverend Leon Sullivan to its board, there was a consensus on the need for greater recognition of blacks throughout the organization. Without an assertive advocate, it would have been difficult to accomplish. Any situation in which an imbalance needs to be redressed may justify constituency representation for an interim period, but that does not mean that a board consisting predominantly of advocates for special interests is desirable or even workable.

No doubt the demands for interest group or quasi-constituency representation stem from the perceived hesitancy of business leaders to deal straightforwardly with the moral and social aspects of business activities. And the perception is correct—there is indeed a reluctance by business boards to challenge established practices or to respond to changing public expectations. Business conservatism runs deep and strong. Unless, under the board chairman's encouragement, a spirit of facing up to new problems can be activated among board members, it may be desirable, even necessary, to add an interest group representative to serve for a period as a "catfish in the herring tank." In the long run, however, a board consisting of members serving specialized interests could not be expected to foster the well-being of the total enterprise.

Indeed, public pressure for greater independence in board members seems to have led some companies to accept the notion of the specialized representation of groups such as women, ethnic minorities, consumers, *et al.* The argument has been developed that all the major social groups affected by a business corporation should have representation on its board and that it is actually to the advantage of a corporation to have first hand access to representatives of the major currents of contemporary society. Yet it is not clear how the interests of multiple, sometimes political, and even opposing constituencies can, in the long run, be reconciled with the best interests of a company. Granted that the public's sanction of the corporation as an economic entity depends ultimately on the approval of a broad range of interest groups in the community, the board is still not called on to become a legislative assembly. In its own interests, it should be more concerned with the general community than it has been, but the corporation cannot be effective if it becomes an arena to test the opposing views of contesting political constituencies.

Effective specialized representation by its nature would end in political conflict on the board and make action in the company's interest more difficult. Indeed, effective service to a particular group may create a conflict of interest with the institution the board member is elected to govern. Over time, all the interests of the separate parties directly or indirectly affected by the enterprise will be best served by its balanced and healthy total development.

This is not to say that specialized interests should go unsponsored. With an appropriate degree of independence, all members of the board could be expected to espouse special causes from time to time, and not just the causes of their own socioeconomic group. All who are worthy of board membership could be expected to do this, regardless of their sex, race, religion, or ethnic background. The intelligence, knowledge, and character of the director should be paramount in board work. It is the task of the chairman to encourage the free expression of those qualities in the interest of the total enterprise. That will better solve the company's problems than the device of selecting directors simply because they represent a particular segment of society.

The notion of selecting members of the board to represent nonspecific interests—consumers in general or the community at large—seems even less promising. A basic difficulty, of course, is the matter of selection. Everyone is a consumer and a member of the public. The consumer and public community can become very large indeed in the case of the corporation whose activities cover the nation or the world.

One can logically ask, moreover, whether special interest directors, including labor representatives, would be concerned with the impact of the corporation on the community at large. The assertion of the special group self-interest seems more likely, and the corporation could be seriously hurt. In the opinion of Professor Phillip I. Blumberg, it

> . . . would transform the board into a political institution, a microcosm of the community. All the directors would become, in effect, special interest representatives (whether for an outside group or simply for the stockholders), working to satisfy their particular constituency. The problem of conflict of interest for the individual board members would be replaced by the problem of conflict among the directors. It is extremely doubtful that such a board could manage a corporation effectively. Board decisions would involve shifting alliances between constituent groups, with log rolling deals (for the exchange of support for respective proposals), all of which would lead to a condition described by Beardsley Ruml decades ago as "gangsterism." [6]

At present, only rarely have those representing blacks, women, former government officers, etc., on boards of directors had significant business experience in their backgrounds. That does not necessarily destroy their usefulness as board members. If they are able to relate to the needs of the company and if their perception of external influences that will

50

affect its future is sharp, they can make worthy contributions. People with quite different backgrounds can bring a useful perspective to board deliberations, *if they place the interests of the company first.* Other nonbusiness persons who have frequently been invited to boards are from the fields of education, usually academic administrators, and occasionally, from the military, medical, writing, and more rarely, clerical professions.

Although it is not a good reason by itself, adding nonbusiness people has a positive public relations value. There is a clinging public skepticism of the ability of business to understand the needs, or even be aware of the aspirations, of politically potent elements of society. Additions to the board from such groups may help to forestall mandated representation.

Stockholder Democracy

What could be more plausible than stockholder democracy? Who could be against it? We have citizen democracy in politics. Ultimate power is said to rest in the people, and politicians tend to respond to public desires. Why shouldn't corporate managers similarly be required to respond to the desires of stockholders, the ultimate owners? Why isn't it feasible to design more effective corporate devices to make the wishes of stockholders felt, comparable to the political arrangements that are said to assure responsiveness in politicians?

The analogy has strong appeal at a time when public approval of business is at a low ebb. The Senate Commerce Committee has held hearings on the issue of making corporations more accountable to their stockholders and to the public. In June 1978, the SEC was considering changes in its proxy rules about stockholder communications. It had held public hearings that centered on stockholder communications. The Federal Trade Commission has also demonstrated an interest. Even private groups such as the American Law Institute, the New York Stock Exchange, the Business Roundtable, and the American Assembly have entered the debate.

Corporate management has made efforts to be aware of, and within the constrictions of a balanced policy, responsive to, the dominant desires of stockholders. This is not unlike the effort to achieve a certain harmony between the policies of government and the preferences of the people at large. But so general an observation when applied to the corporation begs the issue of leadership, obfuscates the legitimate claims of other interests, and assumes widespread understanding by an informed majority of stockholders of highly complex matters. Moreover, on closer examination, the comparison of corporate responsiveness to stockholders with that of government to its citizens is less meaningful than it may seem at first blush. A dissatisfied stockholder can sell out; a dissatisfied citizen by and large cannot. There are many indirect stockholders, members of pension trusts, mutual funds, etc. However, there are no "indirect citizens." In a democracy, citizens have equal status, one-man–one-vote; stockholders do not.

Moreover, many political observers have concluded it is only partly true that governmental policy is the result of public opinion. Rather, in a democracy as well as in totalitarian societies, it often appears to be the other way around: public opinion seems to follow political leadership. The main restraints on political action usually are not provided by a clearly articulated majority opinion; rather they stem from countervailing group pressures and from the constitutional requirements of periodic elections. Moreover, a continuing bureaucracy determines much governmental policy and is sluggish in responding to unwanted pressures. Thus, an attempt to model the actions of corporate managers on those

52

of government officials should be preceded by a careful examination of their respective purposes and positions. They are only partially comparable. The specious analogy that has been developed by critics of the corporation would seem to have usefulness mainly as a form of political persuasion to convince the public that more control must be exercised over corporate management.

It has been said many times, in the interest of the business corporation, that management must find means to become more aware of the aspirations of the public. But the political device of *stockholder* voting to register *public* attitudes may be the least effective way to achieve that result. In fact, it could be counter-productive, for the interests of stockholders in a particular company may be narrowly conceived and antithetical to the public interest.

More than four decades (1932) ago Adolph A. Berle, Jr., and Gardiner Means, in their famous book *The Modern Corporation and Private Property,* identified the separation of beneficial ownership of the corporation from effective control. The nature of the stock company, they said, had split the atom of private property. On balance they felt the consequences to be pernicious. Just as strong a case, perhaps a stronger one, can be made that it was a constructive development. It facilitated the development of the system of management that could exercise stable continuity of control and the emergence of a new class of highly trained and professional managers. A sense of stewardship now present in the business community, although not widely perceived, is the foundation on which new conceptions of purpose are being built in the business world.

Realistically defined, the stockholder's interest is simply to receive as quickly as possible the largest return on investments consistent with a given level of risk. The professional manager, on the other hand, is more interested in the development of the enterprise through time, although he (or she) is keenly aware that a person's career will ordinarily be judged by financial results over short periods of time. The directors, unlike the managers, are the best positioned to mediate these two interests and design the corporation's long-range success.

If a significant degree of discontent exists among stockholders today, it is more related to the level of dividend payments and to the behavior of share values in the open market than to the detailed nature of corporate operations. There is little evidence that they seek a bigger piece of the management action. Some stockholders, of course, have properly objected to undisclosed foreign payments and illegal domestic payments. Interestingly enough, however, others have criticized the government for disadvantaging businesses by interfering in these practices, long-established in other countries. But the idea of polling stockholders to determine attitudes with respect to most matters relating to corporate operations might properly be described as an imaginative remedy seeking a problem. If the vote is based on one-investor–one-vote the task would be clumsy and slow, as well as usually uninformed. If the vote would, in any case, reflect the views of the larger investors, a few phone calls to large institutional holders would settle a question.

Minority stockholder groups have used the proxy machinery as a form of stockholder democracy to object to some matters or espouse others. Minority stockholders, representing church groups, public interest groups, and others have used the proxy as a device to influence corporate decisions. Pressures to withdraw investments and jobs from South Africa and Angola are current examples. But one might well ask, is it politically desirable or effective for citizen groups to apply clout through the corporation rather than directly through their government?

The investment and financial relationships between stockholders and management is a more direct matter and has a well-known legal history. It has long been the focus of cor-

porate law. Numerous past abuses, with management bene-
fitting itself at the expense of stockholders, have been identified and some remedial action has been taken. Devices to
secure control of a company through the issuance of class B
or other kinds of stock, with unusual and discriminatory
voting rights but limited capital contributions, have had the
attention of the New York Stock Exchange. Stock options
granted to management on advantageous terms have now
been surrounded with constraints. Progress has been made in
protecting dissenting minority stockholders in mergers or in
"buy back" operations that convert a public company into a
private one. But management itself may still be overly protected in its ability to secure its jobs by blocking a merger
that may be otherwise advantageous to stockholders. Newly
legislated limitations on the size of executive pensions and
the recent rulings of the Internal Revenue Service place
additional prohibitions on management's perquisites.

Stockholder-manager relations appear to have been the
focus of those interested in federal corporate charters or a
federal minimum standards act. Allegedly they are interested
in shielding the stockholder against the sometime cupidity of
management. But the issues of the future are much larger.
It is not just a matter of the relative claims of stockholders
and management. Measures dealing with these issues are less
needed today than before the enactment of state regulations,
the rulings of organized exchanges and the SEC, and judicial
opinions that have tightened the relationship. More can, and
should be done, but new legislation is not necessarily required. Moreover, chartering or legislative processes by their
nature, insert a degree of undesirable rigidity. If, in addition,
a federal charter should require an administratively designed
license to do interstate business, the range of possibilities
would place alarming powers in the hands of government
officials, whose attitudes toward business have seldom been
conspicuous for benevolence.

Corporate managers, despite the legal ambiguities, have acquired quasi-constituencies in addition to stockholders. They are—to repeat—their customers, employees, communities, governmental agencies, yes, even the public at large. To assure the longevity of the business corporation as a vital institution, management must be sensitive to all their claims. Failing to recognize the legitimate requirements of employees or adulterating the quality of products could perhaps produce greater immediate profits for stockholders but in the long run would not serve the interests of anyone, including stockholders. In a real sense these other interests compete with stockholders for attention. To increase the influence of stockholders could, and probably would, simply circumscribe the opportunities of management to run the corporation in the larger world. If the desired objective is to enlarge the legitimate purposes of the corporation to live well in that world, sponsorship of more stockholder democracy is not the effective way to do it.

Ethical Conduct in an Immoral World

Ethics is a word often used but less often defined. It helps us define the desirable in general without saying what the desirable may be in a particular case. Standing alone it often sets forth what is intangible, tenuous, even ethereal, except perhaps to the one who is using the term. A dictionary definition identifies ethics as that part of philosophy dealing with moral conduct, duty, and judgment. In each of the many basic ethical systems, philosophers give these three terms different meanings. Thus a hedonist and a utilitarian would have different meanings for "moral conduct," "duty," "judgment," and a wide variety of other ethical terms.

The difficulty of securing agreement on ethical matters is notorious. Even well-informed persons working from the same ethical premises frequently manage to come up with differing conclusions about what it would be right to do because different attitudes and commitments make them differently evaluate the particular circumstances within which a decision must be made. Thus, depending on the circumstances, commitments, and attitudes of an individual, his judgment may prescribe one course of action and his sense of duty may prescribe another. Witness the influence payments made to foreign government officials and the illegal domestic political contributions by leaders of American corporations. Corporate officers presumably felt that their duty to the company overruled their judgment that to make payments was wrong.

And ordinary mortals rarely think about ethical matters from a consistent ethical stance. Their ethical conclusions are usually the result of imperfect inferences drawn from assumptions taken from different ethical systems. The result is added complexity and more difficulty in securing agreement.

Another definition of ethics is conformity to formal or professional rules of right or wrong that describe a system of conduct. Several decades ago Walter Lippman made an interesting and convincing case for a code of personal behavior acceptable to society. He called it "the Public Philosophy." Codes of conduct do exist in the professions of law, medicine, and others. Many business corporations have long had codes of conduct, and more have been added in recent years—and are still being added—to govern the activities of their members. Few such codes, however, have survived since the days of the NRA (National Recovery Act) when many were designed to cover entire industries.

In connection with the public perception of business codes, an assumption widely held for many years may be gradually weakening. Businessmen, engaged in activities for a profit, it has been believed, are more tainted with self-serving than doctors, lawyers, clergy, academics, government officials, and others in the not-for-profit sectors of society. The author's observation over many years provides convincing evidence that this simply is not so. All are self-serving to one degree or another, and businessmen not discernibly more so than those in other professions.

External restraints are required to supplement self-restraints on people in the everyday walks of life. The behavior of professionals is no exception. Examples are abundant. Until recently, doctors severely limited entry into their profession; the result was that medical fees escalated far more rapidly than other components of the cost of living. Lawyers, in a recent antitrust case, presented a legal bill in excess of $30 million that was found by the court to be too high and subsequently reduced to $8 million. The academics find their main satisfactions in activities that bring psychic income beyond financial rewards, but often follow procedures that are archaic and inefficient. The rumble resulting from an attempt to update an archaic curriculum bears witness to how highly cherished is the time that is spent on acquisitive activities, which should be devoted to keeping up with the literature in their field. Government officials work at a deliberate pace, look for ways to line their pockets, and manifest a conviction of the rightness of their use of power usually shared by few of the citizens they serve. No—businessmen as individuals are neither more nor less moral or avaricious than other professionals. Moreover, they are less contentious among themselves. For the most part they get along very well with each other and are able to achieve consensus far more readily than those in other professions.

The image of business leaders with the public, however, is none too flattering. They are regarded as strong, hardheaded, ambitious, and unrestrained by higher moral considerations in their business relations, even though in other matters they are perceived to be as moral as the rest of society. Thus, the "off-book" payment disclosures by otherwise law-abiding corporate officers is seen by business critics as a reflection of the immorality of the business world.

At least part of the explanation can be found in the

contrast between individual morality and group morality. Whether written or not, each group in society has its own code of conduct that imposes in direct and subtle ways on its members. The corporation is no exception. Even though the code of the corporation is now in a stage of transition, the conduct of most of its present leaders could not fail to have been conditioned by circumstances that existed during the period when their careers were fashioned.

The late Clarence Randall, an outspoken business leader several decades ago observed,

> Free enterprise as we practice it in the United States is authoritarian in principle. One man decides—the will of one man is the activating force—he speaks and others obey.[7]

That one man usually has been schooled in the belief that only one thing counts, the net profits of the enterprise, and that the corporation has but one constituency, the stockholders. Nothing else matters, even if law is occasionally bent or even broken to achieve the goal. Why otherwise would competent and intelligent executives have risked, and indeed lost, their careers with no prospect of significant personal gain?

The careers of most of the present generation of business leaders began with these narrow premises unquestioned. Once in the corporation and its authority accepted, reciprocity in the form of security and protection can become comfortable. Conformity and obedience to those senior in the hierarchy seem a modest price to pay for the opportunity of career progress, and a moral man or woman will only occasionally find matters that conflict with his or her personal standards of conduct. Acceptance of company goals and obedience to those who interpret them becomes a way of corporate life. Until recent years, those goals have all targeted on the single purpose of making money, as much as possible as quickly as possible. Having spent a lifetime in that environment, a present incumbent of the combined office of chairman and chief executive officer could not be expected to change the rules of the game. Public relations statements and intermittent societal programs to the contrary, basically the rules have remained the same for the devotees of "the Old School."

Will the off-book payments and similar practices be resumed, once public indignation has died down? No one knows for sure. Perhaps they will, despite the newly drawn corporate codes of conduct. Strong pressures to succeed are still in place, and typical chief executive officers are so committed to traditional expectations that they may be willing to risk a career if that seems necessary. Greater loyalty hath no one! But is it duty? Is it the right kind of loyalty to the firm? How confused and frustrated those caught in the net must feel! In any case, it is certainly bad judgment. However, if, as, and when, corporations progressively abandon the authoritarian principle of one-man rule, as policies are determined on a broadened basis, the satisfactions and benefits of a business career could be still further enhanced, and such temptations could become less appealing. Business life could become more rewarding in all aspects.

Progress has already been made. The new, broadened concept of corporate purposes cannot fail to mitigate the sharp edges of bottom-line compulsions, even though they will still be felt, and properly so. A clearer, more impressive image of business and of the businessman will emerge. A recurrence of successful careers sacrificed without personal benefit would be unlikely simply because the goals of the corporation would be broadened and redirected.

Yet external restraints to supplement self-restraints will always be appropriate for the businessman, just as they are for all human beings. A corporate structure of checks and balances is the logical means of creating them. In matters relating to executive salaries, perquisites, and conflicts of interests, self-restraint is not enough. These things should not be self-determined. A strong and independently minded board of directors should be prepared to exercise jurisdiction in an objective manner after considering all the circumstances, including the competition for executive talent. In a comprehensive sense, senior executives should be protected as much as possible from excessive tension and physical strain so that they can conserve their energies to concentrate on company affairs. The control of deviant practices in salaries, perquisites, and conflicts of interests is easily accomplished by an effective board, but it should be done with both firmness and understanding of all the circumstances. It is a task better assigned to those who know the company, the personnel, and its industry, than to external governmental agencies.

In all questions having ethical aspects, such as advertising, environmental protection, the movement of manufacturing plants out of communities or overseas, or personnel discrimination, the solution is likely to be most rational if developed within a corporate structure of checks and balances. Externally imposed solutions, however, will inevitably make their appearance if the problems are not handled well internally. And those solutions will inevitably and invariably be less rational.

There is no reason to believe that personal morality is higher in government or in the professions than it is in business. The important thing is to provide within the corporate structure effective disincentives to behavior that is antisocial. Departures from what is regarded as moral conduct are found in all phases of human existence, and should be identified and penalized wherever they appear. But the building of a tradition within the corporation of integrity and ethical conduct, together with a system of internal checks and balances, provides a greater assurance of public protection than chaperonage by those external to business, many of whose personal behavior itself has failed to qualify for that role.

Notes

1. Paul Weaver, "Corporations are Defending with the Wrong Weapons," *Fortune* (June 1977).

2. *Ibid.*

3. Gerstacker, from a message to stockholders, Dow Chemical Company.

4. Lionel Trilling, cited in *Columbia Today*.

5. Arthur Okun, talk to Economic Club of Chicago, October 1977.

6. Phillip I. Blumberg, "Who Belongs on Corporate Boards?", *Business and Society Review*, No. 5, Spring 1973, pp. 40–47.

7. *Folklore of Management* (1959), p. 28.

4

Real Issues

O<small>F</small> all the issues that have become more—rather than less—confused with the passage of time, the standouts are antitrust policy, competition, and inflation. Sometimes they are viewed separately, sometimes as interrelated. Antitrust legislation and administration had its genesis in both classical economic theory and in nineteenth-century populist politics. In some respects, these dual roots were antithetical. On the one hand, competition was deemed to be good, for it would assure technological progress that would result in better products at ever lower prices. On the other hand, too much competition was felt to be bad, especially if the advantageously situated big corporation drove out its smaller competitors.

These opposing purposes of the antitrust program have never been generally understood. The position is not now uncommon that antitrust laws, originally intended to promote consumer welfare, have been converted into a mass of restrictions on competition that permit exploitation of the consumer. And the line between "good" and "bad" competition, fuzzy at best, has shifted from time to time. Moreover, administrative agencies and the courts have moved their positions with the dominant public concerns of the time. Finally, these shifting attitudes toward competition have done little to dampen inflation, and, indeed, they may have contributed to it.

Competition and Antitrust Policies

At the turn of the century, the major concern in antitrust affairs was consolidations and mergers. This was followed by public focus on "cutthroat" tactics, rebates, and discrimination. Then followed concern about financial controls and interlocking directors. Domination of industries by single corporations or by small groups of corporations called oligopolies, then occupied public attention. Now "shared monopolies" are at center stage. But despite three-quarters of a century of legislation, administrative rulings, judicial opinions, and scholarly literature, the terms monopoly and competition still lack precision.

Theoretical concepts of pure or perfect competition, imperfect competition, and monopolistic or oligopolistic competition have failed to provide adequate guidance for the achievement of socially desirable results.[1] The only thread of concern consistently reappearing in the literature, legislative enactments, and judicial rulings has been a suspicion of bigness. Yet the public has continued to accept and patronize the large business corporation, both as investors and as customers. A concept of "workable competition" seems to have emerged without the enthusiastic support of scholars or the legislative guidance of politicians. A "workably competitive" economy has provided an enlargement of consumers' choices at increasing real values—without the exploitation of the public. Otherwise, the rate of return on invested capital would have increased instead of decreasing—as it has.

In recent times antitrust activity has tended more to contribute to price maintenance and the prevention of price discrimination than to promote better products at lower prices. Price cutting by large corporations especially has been regarded as undesirable discrimination. Yet price mainte- nance, whether in the cost of products or of labor, deprives the nation of a principle defense against inflation. No topic is more conspicuously current than inflation, yet public pro- nouncements by academic, political, business, and media leaders have left the public puzzled as to its root causes and persistence.

The subject of competition is usually discussed by econo- mists and legal scholars in terms of behavior that departs from a theoretical model of so-called perfect competition. It is alleged that corporate managers can set prices, under oligopolistic or monopolistic conditions, that are not related to supply and demand or to unit costs. Without defining "monopoly", or its counterpart, "competition", the Congress passed the Sherman Act in 1890, proscribing combinations in restraint of trade, monopolization, and attempts to monop- olize. In 1914 the Clayton Act restrained mergers, trade tie- ins, and exclusive dealing arrangements that might substan- tially lessen competition or tend to create a monopoly. Both laws aimed at preserving the competitive motivation to inno- vate and to assure product improvement that would be passed along to the consumer in ever better values.

As is so often the case, the best of intentions can have perverse results! Many mergers at the turn of the century have been left undisturbed, presumably in recognition of the economies of scale that were achieved in these cases. The Justice Department, the Federal Trade Commission, and the judiciary through the years have been somewhat more toler- ant of vertical mergers, that is, integration from raw material to finished products, than of horizontal mergers that have involved the risk of the cartelized practices of sharing or allocating the market of homogeneous products, price con- spiracy, and uniform specification agreements.

The 1950 Cellar-Kefauver Amendment to the Clayton Act, however, attempted to proscribe all corporations from combining their interests, either through stock or asset acquisition, whether horizontal or vertical combinations, even if the result should be economies of scale. Michael Pertschuk, the current Chairman of the Federal Trade Commission, has been quoted by the *Financier* to the effect that:

> There are always going to be trade-offs, and there may very well be situations where greater efficiency—carrying with it, perhaps, lower prices—should yield to other social objectives.[2]

In the meanwhile, the current conglomerate merger wave, which is seldom accompanied by significant economies of scale or job-creation, is relatively unimpeded by antitrust legislation and adjudication. Indeed, impairment of economic efficiency may well be the price the nation is paying for what is believed to be the pursuit of industrial competition by the protection of competitors.

Having accepted the classical economists' definition of perfect competition and finding it unattainable, and realizing the subsequent theoretical constructions to be of limited use, we seem to have lost confidence in the ability of competition to do its work, that is, to make goods and services flow through market choices toward the most productive use of resources. We have come to prefer administrative and judicial decisions as to how production should be organized instead of reliance on the market to allocate resources and induce production to conform to consumers' desires.

The literature regarding antitrust is voluminous, though more instructive than enlightening. Markets are defined narrowly and the percentages held by specific sellers are studied. Instead of appraising the ability of competition to provide increasing real values through time, which it has done, observers study short-term price behavior. There can be no compromise with conspiratorial practices to fix prices and share markets, but what has been described as the "ruck of legalistic bickering and economistic thumbsucking" has no contribution to make to public well-being. Rather than starting with the ancient postulates inherited from another day, or with the array of accumulated literature and legislation, or with administrative and judicial rulings that are often shiftingly ambiguous or incompatible, the presidentially appointed National Commission for the Review of Antitrust Laws and Procedures could have based its studies on the hard realities of a complex economy. Its contribution to the public welfare would have been more significant than that of the Temporary National Economic Committee of 1938. Unfortunately, that has not been the case.

Still other features of our antitrust policy and administration are of dubious value; indeed, they may be contraventions of the public interest. Before reciting them, however, it should be emphasized that without the constraints of competition sought through antitrust or other comparable law, something would have to take its place. Minimizing the barriers to new entry is perhaps the most promising. The maintenance of an appropriate degree of competitive discipline is essential to curb cupidity in all phases of human activity. That is one of the basic lessons to be learned from nature, and it is particularly true of the business community, even though business rivalry must be tempered with a sense of social justice.

Nevertheless, antitrust law is in urgent need of repair. Among the programs of antitrust that appear to be of doubtful desirability are the current "big company suits" that seek divestiture. These suits are sometimes brought by government and sometimes by private competitors. Several current cases are horrendous examples of wasted resources. Five years passed in pretrial and trial proceedings after the case of *SCM vs. Xerox* was filed. Damage claims of $500 million were sought. The *pretrial* documentation alone came to about 96,000 pages, which bulked roughly 20 feet thick. There were

215 trial days, with 41,000 pages of testimony recorded. The cost to the litigants was said to exceed $60,000,000.[3] a jury verdict has now been rendered, setting damages at $11,730,874, practically all of which Xerox has petitioned the judge to set aside.

Or again, recognized as a quasi-monopoly and therefore subject to the regulatory procedures of the Federal Communications Commission, the American Telephone and Telegraph Company nevertheless some four years ago was made a defendant in a suit the purpose of which is yet to be precisely clarified—presumably divestiture of Western Electric, its Long Lines Department, and other assets. After four years of mutually contested legal discovery proceedings, the trial has yet to begin. And there are even worse performances. Five years of pretrial proceedings have now passed before trial has commenced in the so-called "shared monopolies" cases of four companies in the breakfast cereal business; and, in another case, six years of pretrial proceedings elapsed before trial of eight integrated oil companies. But the International Business Machines case is the classic. Trial finally began after nine years of preliminaries outlasting six Attorneys General, the substitution during the period of several teams of government lawyers, and a complete change in the nature of the company's products. IBM has become a new business since the case was started. Not one of its present products was on the market when the suit began, and its prices, related to performance, have declined dramatically. The principal interests served by these cases are those of the legal profession—not of the general public.[4]

The most authoritative and at the same time the most devastating appraisal of big company antitrust cases is attributed to the present head of the Antitrust Division of the Justice Department, Mr. John H. Shenafield:

> . . . the theoretical and sometimes rubbery concepts of antitrust law seem ideally suited to endless searches down

barren back alleys for testimony that does not stand witness to anything, for mountains of documents that do not prove anything, and for abstruse briefs in support of legal theories that do not mean anything.[5]

Apart from the vast expense and commitment of legal talent assigned to these exercises, the results are of doubtful value. The competitors of IBM, and seemingly the Antitrust Division, would be happy if the company brought fewer new products to market and charged higher prices. It is interesting to note that in the recent Eastman Kodak case the jury severely penalized the company *because* it innovatively brought out the Instamatic camera—not because it was withheld from the market. Hard though it may be to believe, legal fees in excess of $30 million (later reduced to $8,000,000 by the court) were presented to Eastman by the successful plaintiff, based on some 83,000 hours of legal work at $350 an hour! The only major recent case of compelled divestiture has been Kennecott's sale of Peabody Coal. It required a joint venture of large corporations to buy the property— which neither enhanced competition nor satisfied the Federal Trade Commission.

In the hands of legislators, lawyers, and judges, antitrust law has become more a means of protecting competitors from "unfair competition" than of enhancing competition. The premise seems to be: the more competitors the more competition, even if the most efficient is compelled to protect the less efficient by withholding its comparative advantage from the consumer. This is an inversion of the original spirit of the antitrust movement, which was to assure that the benefits of efficiency were passed along to the public.

Solicitude for the small merchant and for his preservation in the chain of distribution was recognized some years ago by lawyer-dominated Congresses in the passage of the Robinson-Patman Act of 1936, which limited price differentials within a trade and the Miller-Tydings Act of 1937, which sanctioned resale price maintenance. Both exempted specific actions, in certain circumstances, from the initial spirit of the anti-trust laws, and, in fact, denied the right to unbridled competitive price behavior as disturbing to the normal channels of distribution. Even though Miller-Tydings was repealed several years ago, there will no doubt be "fair trade" measures modifying antitrust law taken in the future to assure orderly markets or to protect those conceived to be disadvantaged in the competitive race. The states even now have numerous laws that restrict advertising, limit entry by prescribing licensing, and otherwise restrain competitive practices, particularly among the professions. These are under attack by the Federal Trade Commission, but the states' attorneys general are resisting. Solicitude for the less efficient is in harmony with the groundswell of change now occurring in social values, a change toward greater collaboration and compassion and away from the postulates that underpin the unqualifiedly competitive libertarian economy.

Inflation and the Pass-Through

There is one area of antitrust policy where a shift could and should occur in the direction of tightened control. It has direct relevance to the issue of inflation. First we should note that sustained inflation did not start with the Vietnam War, as so often is thought. It started in the decades of the 1930s and 1940s. Its roots were firmly planted in the public concerns that emerged during the Great Depression. The human suffering associated with that punishing period focused public policy on measures to assist the disadvantaged: farmers, unemployed youth, and the elderly, for example. And among the groups identified for additional assistance was organized labor.

When the Sherman Act was passed in 1890, organized

labor was just as much subject to its antitrust provisions as were corporations. The Clayton Act of 1914 attempted to adjust what was then felt to be labor's relative weakness by exempting the right to organize from antitrust law. The Wagner Act of 1935 provided the right to strike and limited the federal court's injunctive authority to restrict or deny strikes. By the mid-1930s, the right to organize and the right to strike were firmly established and exempt from antitrust law.

In combination with labor's exemption from antitrust, the nation's post-Depression commitment to full employment, epitomized by the Full Employment Act of 1945, made continuous inflation inevitable. With labor's firmly established muscle at the bargaining table, there has been little more than the appearance of resistance to excessive wage settlements. With wage patterns established, the wages of nonunion workers have been similarly adjusted. The risk of "pricing labor out of the market" has been diminished if not eliminated by the confidence that subsequent compensating actions will be undertaken by government to support the commitment to full employment.

The result for three decades has consistently been wage increases greater than increases in productivity, as measured by output per man hour. Improved fringe benefits have simply enlarged the gap. Wage and benefit increases unmatched by increased output per man-hour must necessarily result in higher unit costs of production, which, if uncompensated by higher prices, result in a squeeze of profit margins, declining activity, and unemployment.

The shift of a large part of the labor force from manufacturing to service activities has further exacerbated the situation. Productivity increases in the service areas are both more difficult to achieve and harder to measure. Yet the patterns set in negotiations with the large production and mining unions have become the guides to the settlements in the service sector, especially among the now highly organized teachers, police, firemen, and sanitation workers.

There are those who would hold that the size of wage increases is less relevant or even irrelevant when the economy is operating at less than full capacity. Higher wages create higher purchasing power, and a higher level of consumption is expected to induce greater production, which would spread fixed overhead costs over the greater number of units produced, all of which results, it is said, in a compensating offset of unit costs. The theory would be applicable in a perfectly competitive economy and in one where consumer expenditures bear a constant relationship to personal income. But the facts of the economy's behavior have been quite different. The increased unit costs resulting from disproportionately higher wage rates have typically been passed through to the consumer in higher prices, confirmed and made possible by fiscal deficits and by accommodating monetary policy to avoid an increase in unemployment.

It is no coincidence that, except for five fiscal years, the federal government, under both Republican and Democratic control has run deficits, mostly large, in each of the post–World-War-II years. Nor have the concomitant monetary policies been without the several purposes to permit price increases, to facilitate deficit financing of government, and to help assure full employment. Despite this relief, however, the real rate of return on invested capital has declined for a decade. Deficit financing accompanied by slack monetary policies have provided the means to "pass through" the major part of the higher costs in higher prices. Fiscal and monetary policy have not been so much the generator of inflation, as popularly believed, as they have been and are now the accommodation of inflationary pressures that have preceded them. They are the validation of the superior influence of groups with political muscle, particularly of organized labor.

The compassion felt for the working man and the disadvantaged in the early decades of this century has been converted into the assertive cupidity of groups that make it politically difficult, almost impossible, to stop inflation. In contrast to stable or declining prices for most of the nineteenth century, inflation has been persistent since World War II. An elbow break in price behavior occurred with the start of that war, and the upward trend is now accelerating. The 1978 dollar has only about a third of the purchasing power of the 1946 dollar. Fiscal and monetary policy in the light of this history, are now frail reeds on which to lean in the effort to recapture economic stability. The roots of inflation are too deeply embedded.

The rising costs of providing products or services have still other dimensions. The awakened concern for the disadvantaged has resulted in a federal budget that now transfers about $200 billion annually to support welfare, medical assistance, food stamps, unemployment insurance, housing allowances, old age and veterans benefits, civil service pensions, and other measures to alleviate the conditions of individuals exposed to the vicissitudes of a complex society. Groups other than organized labor have emerged to claim their "entitlements." Still other contributors to the increased costs, in addition to labor costs, are the correction of past environmental abuses, and expenses related to compliance with the explosion of regulatory requirements.

Through the payments of taxes, businesses and the affluent —a good number of whom are newly so—have simply served as a partial transmission belt to pay for these rising costs. The other part has been financed by federal deficits and inflation, which is another form of taxation, indeed the most regressive. Without rising prices in these circumstances, there would ensue a decline of profits, reduced business investments and activity, unemployment and a contracted tax base that would have made the government's program prohibitive. Improved technology and human ingenuity have not been able to achieve fully the required compensating rate of productivity improvement.

The additional costs of alleviating social problems, *alone*, might have been carried by the nation without excessive inflation. The *combined* increased costs of social services and labor costs—the latter contribute nationally some 65 to 75 percent of all costs—have made too great a claim on national capabilities. Even though the nation has enjoyed a period of high economic growth, we have made commitments beyond our national means. More claims have been issued than can be redeemed. The Korean and Vietnam Wars simply added to the burden. The politicians for years have promised too much; the excess demand is expressed in inflation.

The end result of our national policies is a built-in, structural generator of continuous inflation that cannot be cured without repairing the structure. At present the nation has too much sail and little anchor. It will be no easy task to reverse these policies, economically or politically. An extended period of economic disappointment with political recrimination may be the prospect. A tax-based income policy that would penalize both labor and the corporation for inflationary wage settlements would help. Other noncompetitive and inflationary forces at work in the economy, however, could readily divert public attention away from the basic issues.

The major virus creating and nourishing the disease of inflation is the failure of collective bargaining to relate wage adjustments to changes in productivity, thus denying the possibility of achieving reasonable stability in the real unit costs of providing services and products. That, and the politically popular but overly generous commitment to assist the less productive groups in society, are the root causes of inflation. The commitment to assist the less fortunate might be accommodated if the above failure of collective bargaining could be corrected, but not if both problems are uncorrected. A recent observation of Dr. Paul W. McCracken in the *Wall Street Journal* of October 19, 1978 is relevant:

> Compensation in the private sector has been moving upward at a 10 percent per year pace. With the 1½ percent per year improvement in productivity of the last decade, we are apparently on an 8½ percent rising trend in labor costs per unit of output. And where labor costs per unit of output go, the price level will not be far behind.[6]

In a comprehensive sense our post-Depression and post–World-War-II political parties have committed the nation to spending beyond its means, and this in a period of rapid economic growth. The prospect of a period of slower growth will make even more difficult the adjustments required to tame the demon of inflation. Moreover claims that have been issued for the future exceed those of the present; and it should be noted that some kinds of welfare adversely affect productivity, thus the ability to provide future benefits. To say the nation needs inspired and courageous leadership is an understatement. Trade-offs must be found to replace the existing policies. Those policies can only lead to social frustration, and to frustration of labor itself.

Disciplining Competition

There has long been evidence throughout society, expressed in a variety of public policies, of a desire to qualify the unmitigated consequences of effective competition. A. D. H. Kaplan saw this clearly in a study for the Brookings Institution a quarter century ago:

> While the Federal Trade Commission Act put limitations on competition only in the sense of excluding unfair competi-

tive practices, subsequent government measures gave security objectives priority over free competition. This change in emphasis is behind the fair trade laws legalizing the fixing of resale prices for retailers, the policy of crop control with a guarantee of parity prices for farmers, the exemption of labor unions from certain provisions of the antitrust acts, followed by compulsory collective bargaining . . . in addition, various forms of special licensing, *tariffs*, and interstate barriers to free business entry became a part of the current system of *disciplining competition*.[7]

All of these public policies represented, and still represent, qualifications of the free market and the open society that emerged concomitantly with the corporation in the age of science and enlightenment. Whether desirable or undesirable is debatable in each instance, but they must be recognized as part of the fabric of contemporary society. Some have been and some will be modified. More regulations to discipline competition have been added since Kaplan wrote—many more. The important matter is that business leaders understand fully the implications of disciplining competition by legislation and regulation, and perceptively adapt their activities and the business corporation, to the extent possible, to a relatively free and open environment in which it must live and prosper.

More particularly, those responsible for the conduct of the corporation in the current period of transition should reflect seriously about the consequences of substantially reducing the compulsions to competitive behavior in any sector of the economy, including their own. One of the most important sectors of the economy, namely labor, now has a major exemption that gives it a quasi-monopolistic position. It would irrevocably commit the nation's economy to political control if business gained comparable exemptions. A modification of the antitrust status of labor, on the other hand, would contribute to the return of a more stable society in which competition could better play its traditional role.

76

Notes

1. Cf. Joan Robinson, *Economics of Imperfect Competition* (1933), Edward Chamberlain, *Theory of Monopolistic Competition* (1933), and Arthur F. Burns, *The Decline of Competition* (1936). These three volumes, together with several essays by Gardiner Means on administered prices, set the pattern of economic thought about competition for several decades.

2. Michael Pertschuk, cited in *Financier*, February 1978, p. 9.

3. *New York Times*, May 30, 1978.

4. An interesting commentary was recently made about the American Telephone & Telegraph and IBM cases by a legislative assistant of the American Society of Mechanical Engineers, Martha H. Frangiadakis:

Within the government, different branches react differently to the problem. The Department of Commerce, for example, warns against the threats to heavy electronics and computer industries from other nations, while the Justice Department is aiming antitrust actions against IBM and AT&T that are designed to make them more competitive but will make them less competitive with Japan, Germany, and other overseas competitors. (*New York Times*, July 30, 1978).

5. *Finances*, February 1978, p. 6.

6. *Wall Street Journal*, October 19, 1978, p. 22.

7. A. D. H. Kaplan, *Big Enterprise in a Competitive System* (Washington, D. C.: Brookings Institution, 1954), p. 232.

PART **III**

Organizing for
Enlarged Responsibilities

5

Authority Based on Consensus

ADAM Smith had an image of "economic man." He wove around the concept of the single enterpriser an elegant, analytically complete model of economic behavior. He happily concluded that the competitive pursuit of enlightened self-interest would result in the greatest good for the greatest number—the "invisible hand" of nature. Much subsequent thinking in economics and business law has been built on the assumption that economic man is still the central focus of society. And the business corporation is frequently interpreted as the single enterpriser just grown enormously larger, even though the increase in size has brought with it intrinsic changes in its character.

The single enterpriser, the partnership, and the business corporation, whether large or small, are alike in that they share the common goals of survival and growth by maximizing financial gain. But unlike these other forms of business, the large business corporation, during its several centuries of existence, has acquired numerous other goals and assignments, some of which are in conflict with each other. In the large corporation, we have a qualitatively more complex organization; large is different, not just in size but in kind.

81

Adam Smith's pleasant harmony between the pursuit of self-interest and the public good has less validity when the financial goals of the large business corporation seem to conflict with the goals of society. The immediate financial power of the large business can threaten the attainment of the goals of society. Its financial interests are determined by the behavior of relative prices in the open market and are not too difficult to perceive. The interests of society, on the other hand, are determined by many factors and are more difficult to perceive and measure.

Two Models of the Corporation: Small and Large

The market is rarely the best guide for the social conduct of the large corporation. Some business actions are now, and will continue to be, the product of political pressures and coercion, or occasionally and preferably, of collaboration with government or other agencies of society.

Much of the confusion regarding appropriate corporate behavior no doubt derives from applying to the large business corporation concepts valid for understanding the single enterpriser, the partnership, and the new or small corporation. Before elaborating this thought, it will be useful to describe succinctly the characteristics of two conceptual models of the corporation, one simply economic and the other socioeconomic.

The *economic model* of the corporation envisages a relatively small organization that will not make a significant impact on the society in which it operates. Without incurring penalties, its managers can cling to one undeviating purpose: making a profit. Their behavior in the open markets for goods or services need only be as competitive as compelled by law, or as the perceived interests of the corporation may demand. The most appropriate administrative structure for this single purpose is the traditional pyramid, with lines of authority set out as clearly as possible, and with a single chief executive officer at the pinnacle of the pyramid. Business law in the economic model will apply more to management's behavior in its relation to stockholders or owners than to society at large.

The *socioeconomic model,* on the other hand, presents quite a different picture. The corporation is large, and its operations make a noticeable effect on the society that gives it legitimacy. Its managers are exposed to public doubt about the use of their acquired power, confronted as they are with the sometimes contradictory pulls of private gain and social purpose. No longer is it acceptable to adopt the single goal of a maximum profit over a short period. Other purposes and other constituencies in addition to stockholders call for recognition. The public is concerned that, when social demands affect stockholders adversely, the societal interest will be subordinated. As a result, corporate law, which still focuses on management's relation to stockholders, has been supplemented with legislative stipulations that determine the corporation's relations with numerous quasi-constituencies: personnel and labor, consumers, competitors, environmentalists, conservationists, and the public at large.

The idea of more responsive managerial policies has received increased attention within many large corporations. This has occurred even though at times such policies may be felt to serve the long-run interest at the immediate expense of stockholder interest. Even the price behavior of the large corporation in the market place differs in degree from that of its smaller competitors. Continuity of good-will with both suppliers and customers to assure prolonged and mutually beneficial relationships is recognized as being more important than the traditional economists' notion that businessmen seek to maximize the return on each transaction.

Basic questions are involved. To what extent should corporate structure and practice be modified to be more sensitive to public aspirations and expectations? What are the risks of impairing efficiency and growth? The question can be asked in another way: what are the respective merits of authoritative versus consensual management for the small and for the large corporation? Chapter 6 will describe some of the structural devices that rapid change in manufacturing processes, communications technology, and more particularly, social awareness is imposing within the large corporation.

One-Man Direction vs. Group Consensus

It is an often heard cliché that no successful business corporation can be run by committees. Someone at each stage of the decision making process must be responsible to decide, must convert discussion into action, and be held responsible for the results. Yet such decisions, when made without the support of prior consensus that emerges from informed group consideration, run the risk of being dominated by personal predilections. They are deprived of the insights of collective wisdom. Nor need prior consensus destroy the ability to act; the administrative practices of some of the nation's largest and most successful corporations have earned the pseudonym of "American Meeting Company" without impairment of their ability for effective action.

It should be recognized, however, that the introduction of consensus management in many cases would involve a reluctant shift of prestige, power, and authority from those who have won the competitive career race for the top. Pluralism in decision making has limited support among the highly motivated and competent. The merits of a concentration of authority, moreover, are noteworthy. It puts in one individual ultimate authority for policy determination and for the initiation and supervision of subsequent action. It streamlines and expedites decision making and helps to assure prompt implementation.

When one person is the senior officer without peer, it is virtually certain that the program and tone of the corporation will become an expression of his or her attitudes and aspirations. The many instances of resultant effectiveness have given wide currency to the belief that a successful company can have but one head. Indeed, this arrangement can be, and has been, beneficial to many companies, and through them, beneficial to the material well-being of society at large. In a reasonably competitive and stable situation, authoritarian management with one boss at the top of well-conceived and organized administrative pyramids has been a major means of achieving efficiency and growth in small- and moderate-sized organizations.

On the other hand, even for single-minded corporations intent on making money, it can be—and on a number of occasions has been—swiftly calamitous. One colossal blunder of judgment can damage an enterprise seriously, even ruin it. It would be instructive to know the extent to which write-offs, ranging in recent years from $100 million to $500 million, originated in the dominant influence of one decision maker. In another type of situation, a chief's prolonged lack of imaginative leadership or judgment can result in an erosion over a number of years of the organization's vitality. In these cases, the chief is not bad enough to let go, but is retained reluctantly. The decline of great corporations, long wanting in inspired leadership, and the sudden unexpected catastrophes of others are all familiar to students of business history.

The advantages of concentrated authority are more likely to be realized in the young and rapidly developing business, especially if the leader is a person of imagination, courage, and energy. The same is true where companies have deteriorated to a point where they need the resuscitation that can be supplied only by a new and strong hand. In both cases, the justification for one-man control stems from particular circumstances—one the development of a new business, the other the rehabilitation of an unhealthy old one. Readiness to take risks and the capacity for quick and decisive action are a sine qua non in both cases, although even here the possibility lurks that the risks taken will be too great and that disaster will result.

The large, mature corporation presents a quite different set of circumstances. Decision making has come, of necessity, to involve large numbers of people. The impact of the decisions cannot but affect both those inside and those outside the company. Indeed, what have come to be called the "externalities" have at the present begun to appropriate the time and energies of key decision makers to a point where the operation of an efficient business can be jeopardized.

Limitations on the Chief Executive Officer

It may be that corporate management in a technologically complex and socially shifting world is getting beyond the capacity of a single—and mortal—chief executive officer. Without the help of independently minded associates, it is becoming an increasingly difficult assignment. Indeed, some of the loneliness felt today by many chief executive officers is the result of formerly close and helpful colleagues becoming subordinates when they assume the top job. In the big leagues of baseball, whenever a line ballplayer is named manager, even in mid-season, the first thing he does is move out on his road-trip roommate. The act dramatizes his separateness —no more "buddies." Corporate big leagues can be like that.

The typical career pattern of a chief executive officer is a progression through the several line and staff functions of one or more corporations. He spends a work-life in doing specific and clearly identified tasks, always with a sharp eye for the bottom line. It is not easy for him to shift his focus to unquantified values and perceptions. It is not easy to guide a business through a successful adaptation to the public's insistence that quality-of-life concerns should have equal influence on corporate practice with bottom-line considerations.

The chief executive officer so conditioned often finds the traditional corporate administrative system of incentives, motivations, and objectives through which business goals are usually translated into operations to be in conflict with the newly emerging social aspirations. On the one hand, there is the need to preserve efficiency and the incentives for growth, on the other, is the need to satisfy new social criteria, many of which call for investing in activities that are, in ordinary economic terms, nonproductive.

Moreover, the chief executive officer's task of running the traditional activities of a corporation can be expected to become more complex with the passage of time, not less. Rapid change in production methods and product composition associated with evolving technology will require new and distinctive executive abilities. Communications equipment and data processing will impose many adjustments. Ingenuity will be needed to assure supplies, to develop appropriate personnel in the context of steadily changing population pressures, and to adapt marketing to global dimensions. Maintaining efficiency will be even more difficult as the patterns of rewards and career development are redesigned to include an assessment of social performance. A chief executive officer's attention will almost certainly be diverted from maximizing net return on invested capital, the classical measure of efficiency. Yet without a thoroughgoing revision of primary assignments, incentives, and corporate policy, the effort to respond to the revised nature of public expectations will be frustrated.

It is clearly preferable for the corporation and for society that the reconciliation of economic efficiency and the newly assertive solicitude for individual dignity and self-realization be made as far as possible through voluntary initiative within the corporation. A realignment of responsibilities and corporate structure will be necessary to assure this result. To the extent that the terms of the reconciliation are imposed on the corporation by external coercion, the results will be debilitating. The dynamic flexibility of the market will become brittle with irrational rigidities. Effective allocation and use of resources will be diminished. Corporations and their managers will be seen as adversaries of the public will. The current low confidence rating of private institutions will be further confirmed.

A New Look at One-Man Control

What is required is a fresh examination of the complex system of corporate governance, including the role of the chief executive officer and his executive associates and particularly their relationships to the board of directors. Among other things, inputs of new points of view will be required in the decision making process. Only through trial and error can a harmonious blend of economic and socio-psychological considerations emerge. Since a system of checks and balances would best assure a viable result, there will be strong pressures to move toward some form of consensus management and away from the traditional pattern, or what Robert K. Greenleaf has identified as ". . . the hierarchical principle that places one man in charge as the lone chief atop a pyramidal structure." [1]

There are other reasons for abandoning the practice of placing "the lone chief atop. . . ." While being "number one" may satisfy his ego, in a very real and humane sense it often produces an abuse to the individual and his family. And the exceptional qualities that led to the appointment are, in time, impaired by exhausting burdens and obligations. Indeed, the typical tenure in the top office is now no more than five years. Moreover, only an extraordinary individual can avoid the corrupting influence of power, authority, and influence that is only cautiously questioned by his associates, if at all. The opportunity to test ideas rigorously in the hot cauldron of debate and persuasion becomes remote. The processes of succession are often painful—even bruising. Finally, power based on appointive authority rather than on persuasion and voluntarily accorded leadership is usually suspect. It is almost always viewed with skepticism by the public, and it simply feeds the challenge to corporate legitimacy.

A shift in the governance of the business corporation toward more consensual decision making is already evident. Boards of directors are becoming more assertive. But more important, and despite the constrictions of corporate law and legal advice, corporation leaders have begun to recognize that stockholders are not their only constituency. The need for broadened consultation has been increasingly felt. The public expects, and managers have begun to accept, an accountability beyond that to stockholders. The profound significance of this may eventually make the "lone chief atop" an anachronism in a large corporation vested as it is with broad social significance.[2] Moreover, where the top jobs of chief executive officer and chairman are separated both should be in the role of reporting to the whole board. Neither should be viewed as subordinate to the other; they simply have different, though interrelated, functions. An illustration is presented at the end of this chapter.[3]

To the extent that the premise is accepted that the corporation must be concerned with *all* the groups affected by its actions, to that extent, corporate leadership must make a judicial determination of how to balance the interests among its several quasi-constituencies. If the interest of one claimant is avowed—and that only one is the stockholder— the other claimants will surely protest and view management with suspicion. In a perfectly competitive market, this problem would not arise, but markets have never been perfectly competitive and never will be. Nevertheless, competition still determines the limits within which management may make its judgments. Without this restraint, the power of management would be awesome. Within the limits prescribed by markets that are workably competitive, judgment is exercised however, and that judgment will be more successful if it grows out of the consensus of an intelligent peer group seeking the long-range interests of the corporation—and the interests of *all* involved. The long-range interest of the corporation is the target—not the particular current interest of any one or several constituencies.

Placing stockholder interests alongside other direct and indirect interests that impinge on the corporation may sound ominous to some. Over short periods, the several interests are more likely to be disparate than convergent. A decision to recognize any one or more interests may seem to be at the expense of others, particularly stockholders. A proposal that management, in its "judicial" decision making, treat all constituencies with *equal* concern at all times would be unacceptable to most stockholders—and properly so. Disapproval would be expressed in numerous ways, the most effective being a withdrawal of their equity capital. But if corporate management succeeds in recognizing its several constituencies in a balanced and sensible manner, a major contribution will have been made to the removal of threats to the future development and freedom of action of the business corporation—that is to say, to the stockholders' long-range interests. The development of employee pension and stock participation arrangements long before the intervention of ERISA and other government programs, the initiatives taken several decades ago to expand corporate financial support for cultural, educational, and medical activities, and the exercise of price restraint at recurrent government efforts to "hold-the-line"—all attest to the growing awareness of corporate management of some of its broader constituent responsibilities.

Perhaps the most effective guide to corporate policy relative to its several constituencies is found in an ancient Latin phrase: *primus inter pares* (first among equals). Robert K. Greenleaf has used this principle to prescribe the relationship of the chairman to other board members and of the president to his immediately associated officers.[4] The principle may be even more useful to describe the relationship of stockholders to other constituencies of the corporation. Stockholders are not the only constituency, as legal fiction now holds. The fact is that other constituencies at different times and in different circumstances do get prior attention. But stockholders cannot fail to come out *primus* when management is committed to the best interests of the corporation, for, in the long run, those interests converge with those of stockholders.

A Strengthened Role for the Corporate Board

The board of directors, the highest level of authority in the organization, is the best place to start in refocusing goals and plans. Board functions are different from those of executive (operating) management, and to the extent it is composed of outsiders, board personnel differ from executive management. It is unreasonable to expect executive managers, whose career success is measured by the return on stockholders' investment, to set socially responsible policy and initiate consequent action that significantly increases cost and lessens profits, even if only for the short run. To pursue such policies usually requires the initiative and encouragement of a board that includes strong outside directors with broad and long-range sights.

Conversely, it would be less than meaningful to assign an initiating role in societal matters to the board without strengthening it vis-à-vis management in policy determination. If board members are to be effective in setting goals in matters of social concern, or if they are to relieve executive management of the chore of representing the company to certain of its several publics, there must be a public recognition that the board does, in collaboration with the senior management, determine company policy and appraise executive performance. Executive management, on the other hand, is the agency that is delegated by the board to make these mutually agreed guidelines effective, subject to board review.

Credibility is hard for any institution to earn and retain. Business is no exception. A board of directors with responsibility for guiding the external relations of a corporation, and manned by persons with diverse talents and backgrounds, including—but not limited to—those with business experience and acumen, is much better positioned to win that credibility. Business has long needed articulate spokesmen who can convey the reality of business to the rest of society in a manner that will be confident and convincing, and who can make clear that an open society in the world of work and in the world of politics are one and inseparable; and that the degree of openness will increase or diminish in both together. There is no more natural or effective place to develop the required knowledgeable leadership for business than in the governing boards of its major institutions.

The implications of these suggested changes will no doubt alarm those whose careers have been conditioned by past and present successes in a relatively unchanging corporate world. It is the basic thesis of this analysis, however, that the corporation is confronted with more than a temporary decline in public approval; that it is being accompanied by the growth of a labyrinth of government controls, that there is evidence of a groundswell of revision in the value structure of contemporary society, and that the peril of failure to adapt innovatively to new public aspirations exceeds the recognized risks of doing so.

Two things must happen before the board of directors can be prepared to accept more complex and demanding assignments: (1) a clarification and acceptance of the board's functions as the active monitor, but not the manager, of the operation of a company; and (2) the recruitment of a diversity of board members, some of whom would have distinguished themselves in careers peripheral to, or even outside, the business community. Neither of these steps will be easy.

Recent federal court cases have dramatically increased the personal liability risks of board members. Some observers feel that the present ambiguity in the conception of the functions of the board of directors may be advantageous—more protective for the board member than hazardous. Indeed, highly regarded law firms have counseled against the framing of a formal set of board functions, presumably because it would provide a legal touchstone for testing board performance. Failure to do so, however, reduces the usefulness of the board and prevents taking advantage of the opportunity— perhaps the only really effective opportunity—for the business corporation to adapt rationally to rising public expectations.

The scope and nature of board functions in each company depends on numerous factors, including the traditions of the company, the personalities involved in it, the nature of the business, and its size. Several general observations can usefully be made, however. The board should be a monitoring body, not an executive one. The operating tasks of management are assigned by the board to the full-time officers of the company. The current practice is to pick the chief executive officer and let him select his senior associates. This arrangement has obvious advantages. There are disadvantages, however, if the chief executive officer prefers associates who are too readily compliant. An alternative is suggested by the practice that has developed in recent years in some companies of establishing an "office of the president" or of the chief executive officer, composed of persons whose exceptional talents are complementary and who, *with board designation,* would relate to one another as peers, even though the president would be "first among equals."

Apart from this there are four broad areas ("the four Ps") central to the company's activities that fall within the monitoring competence of the board: (1) the determination of *policy,* in collaboration with executive management, with regard to both internal operations and external matters, particularly societal matters; (2) the audit or review of management's *performance;* (3) the overview of *procedures* for assuring effective operations; and, finally, (4) the appraisal of *personnel,* particularly in the senior echelons.

Effectively functioning in this manner, a board will be a major influence, indeed, *the* major influence in the conduct of the corporation. It will then have the credibility to represent the company and speak for it, as well as for business in general, in political, academic, intellectual, and communicational circles. The chairman is the logical spokesman, but need not be the only one. The job of spokesman promises to be ever more demanding with the passage of time, and, to the extent feasible, it should be removed without delay from the duties of executive management. Too much executive time is now spent on these external activities at the cost of effective administration. The maintenance of efficiency and growth is too important to be neglected.

There is nothing in these proposals to imply an adversary posture by the board relative to executive management; quite the contrary. Even though the board may be concerned more with external relations and with constituencies other than stockholders, and executive management concerned more with efficiency and the bottom line, both board and management are, or should be, united in making their prime interest the healthy development of the company. Ideally, everyone in the organization has the corporation—and not an identified constituency—as his or her first loyalty, and that includes all board members as well as executives and other employees. Nor is this anything new in corporate practice; the general or total corporate interest has long been the overriding consideration in the annual allocation of corporate resources to the affiliates and departments of diversified or multinational companies.

Composition of the Board

A balanced board would include, in addition to those familiar with the company and its operations, people of distinction in other careers. But recruitment is more difficult than it might first appear. Boards now typically consist of senior officers of the company, including members of the chief executive's office, senior officers of other corporations, investment and commercial bankers, law partners of leading firms—which probably include the firm on retainer to the company—and in some instances, substantial stockholders. Most observers agree that the sources of the present pool of directors should be broadened. In recent years an effort has been made to obtain a diversity of backgrounds by adding one or more women and one or more members of the black community. Occasionally, an academic is included. As boards now function, no excessive demand is made on the time of a member, but those few women, blacks, and academics who have been identified as "board material" have often become quickly overcommitted, and it is doubtful that their influence is very great. They can "wear out" quickly.

A balanced board of working members discharging the complex set of assignments necessary to move the corporation into closer harmony with the ever-changing goals of modern society, yet mindful of the requirements of efficiency and profitability—such a board will require a greater diversity of fresh points of view than has yet been common, and a greater degree of independence of thought and action. That does not mean that the company interest should be secondary to the public interest. Rather it means that a thoughtful board with wide experience, some of it in non-business activities, is best equipped to function in the world of tomorrow. Obviously more time and thought must be committed to the board's work. A sense of meaningful participation—and appropriate adjustments of compensation—are strong inducements for qualified people to give that time.

A start has been made in this direction, but it is only a start. In addition to the usual talents and career experiences now represented on boards, new ones must be found to assure a balanced consideration of the complex issues confronting the corporation. This should not be interpreted to mean that the board should consist of individuals with separately identified constituencies. Nor does it mean that legislative compulsions should shape the composition of the board. Differing backgrounds would simply be a means of bringing a variety of views to issues that impinge on society at large. Talents not now often found on boards, but much needed, are those thoroughly familiar with politics and its processes, historians with the perspective and knowledge of past societal traditions, writers and publishers familiar with leading figures in various fields, and yes, even a minister of religion or a philosopher with roots in the working world.

It is especially important that the board become more sophisticated politically. As James L. Gillies, a member of the Canadian Parliament, said to the assembled American business school deans at their 1977 annual meeting:

> . . . there is a profession of politics and it is a profession different from any other, and I submit it is perhaps one of the

least well understood by businessmen . . . the way in which decisions are reached . . . makes politics so difficult for businessmen.[5]

Decisions in democratic politics are more the result of a workable compromise than of the declaration of truth or goals as perceived by hierarchical heads, although the influence of party philosophy and party leaders is usually of major significance. In contemplating a politically sophisticated board, designed to achieve a socially as well as economically balanced appraisal of corporate policy, it should be understood that its discussions would differ significantly from the characteristic consensus that now prevails in the boardroom. It would not be the consensus that quickly results when it is known that one individual holds final authority.

An individual on the board who can serve as a catalyst of consensus is essential. Logically that would be the chairman. As the senior officer of the board, his encouragement of free and open discussion followed by his guidance of the full board to a consensus—it need not be a unanimous conclusion—would require a unique skill that should be a major consideration in his election to the post. The chairman's tasks of organizing the work of the board, preparing the agenda for and chairing its meetings, and serving as the company's spokesman to its several publics are likely to require much of his time, possibly most of it.

These assignments require talents that may or may not coincide with those possessed by a successful executive manager, and the chairman should, therefore, be relieved of all executive responsibilities. It is not often that both executive and mediational talents can be conspicuously found in a single person, even if serving as chairman *and* as the chief executive officer in a large organization permitted time to do both tasks thoroughly. For the tasks are different: one is operational, the other is conceptual. The job of the chief executive officer is above all to keep the company efficient, profitable, and growing if possible. He is the epitome of the value structure of the age of science and reason on which the business corporation was built. The task of the chairman and his board is to help guide the company to policy positions that will assure public approval and secure its survival as a healthy organization. He is, or should be, the influence that assures a blending of social and economic values. Both the chief executive officer and the chairman have a harmonizing main interest—the health of the corporation per se. Through this division of functions, it is to be hoped that the corporation can find the strength to adapt to the changing world it faces.

A new realization is needed of all factors—both negative and positive—when planning for maximum return on invested capital—the new, long-range social factors and the short-range business ones. In this way self-interest can best be adapted to public aspirations. But this happy result will be difficult without a governance structure that provides for checks and balances. For the business corporation of tomorrow, consensus decision making is as important as its counterpart in the political structure of the nation.

Notes

1. Robert K. Greenleaf, *The Institution as Servant* (Cambridge, Mass.: Center for Applied Studies, 1972).

2. For an elaboration of this point see Courtney C. Brown, *Putting the Corporate Board to Work* (New York: Macmillan Publishing Co., Inc., 1976).

3. Close collaboration and complete interchanges of information between the chairman, or chief corporate officer, and president, or chief operating officer, are essential to a healthy company development. This would be facilitated by an identification of functions and by the assignment of *primary* responsibilities, subject to periodic review by the board of directors. Precise assignment of function should recognize the nature and tradi-

tions of the business, and the personalities involved. An illustrative listing may be helpful.

Chairman (Corporate functions)	*President* (Operating functions)
1. Lead in the organization and the work of the board	1. Operating and capital budgets
2. Design procedures to keep the board of directors fully informed	2. Long- and short-term debt, and cash management
3. Corporate communications	3. Supervision of affiliated companies
4. Press releases and chief spokesman to the public	4. New investments, acquisitions, and divestments
5. Stockholder relations	5. Marketing policies and programs
6. Proxy administration	6. Product development and withdrawal
7. Secretary's office, including contributions	7. Real estate administration
8. Government relations	8. Executive hiring, firing, and assignments
9. Trade association contacts	9. Personnel policies and training
10. Legal affairs	10. Foreign offices
11. Pension administration	11. Inventory control and receivables
12. Insurance matters	12. Internal and external auditing

4. Robert K. Greenleaf, *The Institution as Servant* (Cambridge, Mass.: Center for Applied Studies, 1972), p. 12.

5. James L. Gillies, Beta Gamma Sigma Prize Essay, 1977.

6

Restructuring
the Corporation

Yᴇᴀʀ in and year out, decade after decade, business leaders
have made speeches endorsing enlightened corporate practices. Business associations have unremittingly professed social awareness. But the public has remained unconvinced.
The business community at all echelons below senior management has heard the message, but few regard it as applying to themselves. There is an intractable conviction that
personal advancement will be closely related to financial
success—and particularly by financial results measured over
relatively short periods of time. Motivations and incentives are
geared to ever more impressive income figures. Good works
are hard to quantify and are as yet rarely imbedded in the
procedures for appraising personnel. A gap remains between
the professed social awareness of the front office and what
Professor Kenneth R. Andrews of Harvard has called "the
internal force which stubbornly resists efforts to make the
corporation compassionate." [1]

The concept of more production with less human effort
has been the bedrock foundation on which the corporate
business system has been built. Until recent decades, an increase in the most efficient manner of the production and

distribution of goods and services to meet the changing patterns of public desires, has been the central assignment of business—almost the only one. But the growing public preoccupation with quality-of-life concerns not immediately associated with abundance has begun to involve business in activities that would have been regarded as improper in the past, or even illegal. It is now proving to be uncomfortable. Matters for which business is at best inexperienced, and usually ill prepared, have been thrust into the business orbit.

But the leadership of the business community has become increasingly aware that there is a disharmony in the human environment. The ills of society range from discrimination against minorities in employment, to the lack of meaning in the daily work experience, to conservation of scarce resources, to improving the human environment by reversing past trends toward more thermal, noise, land, water, and air pollution, to the excessive clustering of populations, and to numerous other difficulties that are given daily visibility in the public press. The precise role of business in the alleviation of each of these ills is yet only partially identified. Neither the nature of, nor the outer boundaries of, these commitments have been discerned. But there is a new realization that acting independently, or in collaboration with other business organizations, or with government agencies, the business community cannot avoid becoming increasingly engaged in the mitigation of "nonbusiness" problems.

The Inadequacies of Government

The public has begun to believe that government alone cannot cope with the intractable social problems of the present day. Where efforts have been made at local, state, or federal levels, inefficiency and corruption have frequently appeared. Moreover, some of the worst instances of pollution and profligate resource use have resulted from governmental operations in transportation, the military, urban renewal, and job training. Welfare is one of the most obvious areas of government effort. An amusing, but disheartening, example of government inadequacy was provided by a high government officer's description some years ago of the Great Society's welfare program. After noting that the program involved 170 different federal aid programs financed by over 400 separate appropriations, administered by 20 federal departments and agencies, aided by 150 Washington bureaus and 400 regional offices empowered to receive applications and disperse funds, all supplemented and overlapped by state and local jurisdictions, he described the program in still more vivid terms—this sort of thing, he said, is like trying to feed oats to the pigeons through the mouth of a horse.

Since the 1960s the involvement of the federal government in societal matters has been explosive. The budgets of new regulatory agencies such as the OSHA, ERISA, and EEOC, and of the expanded older agencies such as the FTC, FCC, FDA, and SEC, soared from an aggregate of $1.6 billion in fiscal 1970 to $7.0 billion in fiscal 1977. Estimates of the costs for compliance are astronomical. The Commission on Federal Paperwork has estimated an annual cost of $93 billion for filling out federal forms of all descriptions, or about $450 per capita of the nation's population.[2] In a quarter century, a newly organized Health, Education and Welfare Department has developed some 400 programs to alleviate social ills, built a staff of 1,125,000 functionaries, and acquired a budget of $182 billion.[3] Waste, fraud, and mismanagement in the Department has been estimated by its own Inspector General at some $7 billion.[4]

The activities represented by these figures are in part unrelated to business matters, and, where they are related, they cut across industry lines. But the costs to business of these activities in diverted time, in personnel inefficiency, and in enlarged tax burdens are enormous. The *Code of Federal Regulation* (the *Federal Register*) has expanded to more than 70,000 pages. No one knows how much they may have added to unit costs of production, to inflation, and to our competitive disadvantage in world trade. Many feel that productivity has been seriously impaired. The degree of success of this regulatory edifice varies, but dissatisfaction with it is increasing rapidly, and has already been expressed at the polls. And this protest against the high levels of taxation and rigidly administered controls appears likely to grow.

Government efforts, even when declared as "wars" to alleviate social ills, have been tax-expensive, debilitating, disillusioning, and disappointing. Many people in the government itself have reached the same conclusion. The public has begun to look elsewhere for solutions. In part, this attention is directed to the business corporation, despite the fact that failures to develop enlightened self-regulation by business may have been the chief reason for the design of government constraints. Dr. Henry Kissinger has observed that

> most of the new knowledge, skills and techniques that will be needed by the developing countries in the years to come are in the inventory of private industry.[5]

The same may be said about the mitigation of many domestic social difficulties. Despite a staccato of public criticism, the business corporation is seen as the most efficient organization in society for getting something done, once it commits itself to a task. Business leaders have said nothing in public to discourage this belief; rather, they have encouraged it. But it is not easy to see how social commitment fits into the traditional administrative structure or attitudes of corporate business. It is certainly not a comfortable fit. It does not fit at all into the characteristic pyramidal structure of departments or profit centers.

The Characteristic Corporate Structure

It is useful to recall briefly the typical organization of a business firm. It is a system of sub-structures, usually called departments, each a sub-pyramidal type of organization that in combination builds to the major peak at the chief executive office. It is the kind of structure that dominates all corporate thinking, and against which proposals for change are tested. Yet the methods and procedures of this pyramidal organization are less than adequate to cope with either the technological or societal demands that are currently being made and will continue to be made on the business corporation in the years ahead.

This structure is familiar, with its *line* departments of purchasing, manufacturing, transportation, marketing, and with the *staff* departments of accounting, finance, personnel, public relations, and law. The structure is typical of all manufacturing corporations; it differs in financial and public utility organizations only to adapt to the unique characteristics of the markets in which they operate. Most business organizations are fundamentally alike. Efforts have been made to decentralize authority and responsibility and to use so-called profit centers to make this structure more effective and financially accountable. Individuals in charge of each of the sub-pyramids, or departments, are identified as decision makers within prescribed limits.

This is the structure that has evolved over many years by trial and error. It has produced maximum efficiency in routine and repetitious kinds of operations. In an environment that is competitive above all, it is stable and predictable. Lines of authority are defined, even though some ambiguity remains between operating (line) activities and functional (staff) responsibilities. Associated with this kind of a structure, moreover, is the fact that the control and the incentive

104

systems that are embedded in it tend to inhibit rather than encourage change and initiative. Mr. Theodore Houser, while chairman of Sears, Roebuck saw this clearly more than two decades ago:

> A company with a rigid functional organization, with a highly authoritative line of command for each function, is severely limited in providing a broad program for individual development and advancement. . . . The tendency is to develop rigid areas of control and bureaucratic procedures . . .[6]

Quite apart from social considerations, there are numerous business-related factors, such as accelerating product obsolescence, that have compelled a good deal of structural modification. The urgency of introducing new products is accented as the obsolescence periods for previous ones become shorter. Despite the fact that the amounts spent on research and development have diminished relative to national GNP, they are still large enough to assure a continuous flow of new products. Moreover, markets are rapidly changing. Some are growing, some stabilizing, some contracting, and many are becoming global. Technology is rapidly changing, both in production and in communication.

But the principal compulsions for adaption of an administrative structure come out of the emerging milieu in which business now must operate. Peripheral activities not immediately related to the processing, servicing, and selling of goods and services are appropriating more executive time and attention. Changing corporate behavior must start with top management's breadth of vision and a system of motivating and measuring social as well as economic performance. But it is doubtful that without modifications of the traditional administrative structures, significant change in behavior throughout the organization can be achieved.

New initiatives must be found to make more effective the corporate response to its changing environment. The number of special projects to be dealt with will multiply. Better means must be developed to *anticipate* problems as well as adapt to them after their appearance. New technology, new markets, new analytical methods, and unfamiliar assignments related to the society at large, all will combine to require attention heretofore not characteristic of corporate life. *Flexibility* is the key word. Deeply rooted corporate and personal convictions will be tested continuously. To the extent that management adjusts to these new tasks, a number of divergent procedures and forms of organization will emerge. The tasks that lie ahead for the large corporation are too complex for one man fully to grasp, or even for whole departments as now organized to respond to with comprehensive competence.

Some General Features of Social Commitment

Before examining some of the specific organizational changes that are beginning to appear, it may be useful to look briefly at some of the more general characteristics of these forthcoming societal tasks. First, it should be recognized that the ills of society have a long time dimension. They probably are not going to be cured quickly with or without business participation. They have been with us, in one form or another, as long as recorded history, which means that to succeed in its social purposes, business commitment must be constant and consistent. Participation in community affairs should not be a one-time, some-time, or part-time thing. It is not something to be put on the agenda only in response to intermittent public protest. It is not something to indulge in during good times and then drop in a depression. The commitment of both purpose and corporate resources must be firm and continuous, or it should not be undertaken at all. Continuity is essential.

The classical economists concentrated their attention on the laws of supply and demand as they affected the single transaction. But corporate business is a continuous flow of transactions and of enduring associations. If the element of mutual benefit in the marketplace over time is missing, the flow of goods and services will soon cease and the business relationship will terminate. Just as in strictly business relationships, mutuality and continuity go together in societal affairs. On-again-off-again practices that fail to recognize a continuity in the mutuality of human interests are simply not good business; particularly, it is not good business to fail to see that, in the long run, the interests of employees, the community, and the public at large must be reconciled in a balanced fashion with those of stockholders. This is the essence of enlightened corporate self-interest. In the business of large corporations there is no other realistic choice.

Disappointments are inevitable. Good intent will often be misinterpreted. Indeed, the results of action based on good intentions can prove to be perverse and counter-productive, hence, frustrating. Yet business leaders are properly expected to accept social risks as they have long accepted business risks. It will be in the interest of business to do so.

It is also in the interests of business leaders to speak out frankly and perceptively as they see the public interest, in the conviction that ultimately that interest will coincide with the interests of business. This does not mean limiting business statements simply to defensive responses to accusation of inaction or of unperceptive conduct. Rather it means a positive initiation of opinion about the community interest, despite the risks involved. Businessmen have too long been muted by the conviction, until recently rejected by judicial and administrative rulings, that public issues not immediately related to their specific activities "are none of our business." The practice should be dropped. The business community has its full quota of intelligence; it should be shared in the molding of total public opinion and policy. But that can be effective only if the voice of business carries the unqualified conviction that over time the public and private interests are synonymous.

This seems to have been the opinion of the U.S. Supreme Court in *First National Bank of Boston vs. Pellotti* (1978), which held that corporations have the right of free speech, not merely in their self-interest but in the public interest as well. The long-held dictum that it is permissible for business to speak out on economic issues that affect it, but not on social issues, has now been modified. It must be recognized, however, that business participation in the national debate about issues that are important, but not central, to business, places heavy responsibility on the boards of business companies. Narrowly conceived, self-serving positions can be more harmful than helpful to credibility. Moreover, the problem common to the leaders of all organizations of expressing consensus rather than the predilections of an individual is especially applicable in the case of the corporation.

Business organizations that on balance fail to serve all of their constituencies will not long prosper, regardless of the continuing legal base of stockholders. The notion that other groups affected by business activities cannot be placed on a plane with owners is valid only for short periods of time. Managers who identify the broad public interest and adapt their organizations to that interest will be most assured of enduring success on behalf of their owners. As a Burson-Marsteller report of August 1978 stated:

> When Rachel Carson brought forth *Silent Spring* 15 years ago, her words literally shook the corporate world. That many business executives were totally unprepared for what she had to say gave her message added impact.
> When Ralph Nader attacked the nation's largest automaker with his book *Unsafe at Any Speed*, the impact was far-reaching, too. Again, more so because the community didn't see it coming down the road.
> Here we have prime issues that have affected corporate operations for most of two decades: ecology . . . [and] con-

sumerism. [They] . . . seemed to strike with the suddenness of a tornado along a peaceful country lane, ripping off rooftops and uprooting trees. But did these issues actually emerge from nowhere? Or were there warning signals, blips on the radar screen that everyone ignored?

We suspect the blips were there, but corporate radar watchers were insufficiently attentive. As a result, corporate management was caught off-guard and frequently responded more out of desperation than reasoned thought.

First, industry attacked the conclusions, if not the motives, of people like Miss Carson and Mr. Nader. When that tactic boomeranged, industry began to recite the litany of its accomplishments—how it had mass-produced the nation into the highest living standard in the world. While the recitation was true, it failed to address the problem at hand.[7]

Another general characteristic of the tasks ahead is that *cooperation and collaboration* will henceforth play a larger role in business relative to the concept of *competition*. Barry Bosworth, director of the Council of Wage and Price Stability, has observed that

> most Americans simply do not believe in tolerating the inequities of a "competitive economy," which in any case the country no longer has.[8]

New forms of collaboration between government and business must be found to supplement those already designed. Government in turn, despite the antitrust laws, must find ways to facilitate collaboration *among* business organizations for identified public purposes. In this way the competitive disadvantage incurred in independently undertaken societal activities can be diminished. The functions of trade and industry associations could be enlarged in the public interest, but only with an enlargement of their own vision of their role. The "devil-take-the-hindmost" approach is an unhappy remnant of the nineteenth century in societal matters despite its validity for the open market.

A word of caution must be noted about the social commitment of business. Profitability must be preserved—in the interest of both society and business. A business must operate at a profit or it cannot operate at all. The taxing power belongs only to governments. There is no point to discuss participation in relieving social problems if a corporation becomes unprofitable in its primary mission. Accountancy is a harsh disciplinarian. Indeed that fact is a major source of the strength of business. It is a continuous spur to effectiveness. In their newly evolving posture in society, businessmen must never lose their awareness of the hard disciplines that underpin their past accomplishments and that have made business acceptable to the public despite some conspicuous transgressions.

Nor should the high value on individual initiative and self-reliance be modified, despite some recent tendencies toward inefficient behavior in corporations. Safeguards must be found against the undue impairment of the traditional role of producing and distributing goods and services at the lowest possible unit costs. This primary task must continue to be carried out efficiently to assure the appropriate use of national resources. Despite Mr. Bosworth's observation, the effectiveness of the market economy depends on the maintenance of an adequate degree of competition. That must not be lost. As noted before, "workable competition" stands in contrast to monopoly, on the one hand, and in contrast to so-called perfect competition, on the other.

These are some of the characteristics involved with social performance around which business leaders may arrange their thinking to cope better with the new tasks ahead. Ambiguities will be readily seen: contradictions among quasi-constituents' interests, issues that lie outside business experience, and trade-offs among decreases and increases in unit costs of production.

Finally, with all the problems, one is tempted to ask: why should business involve itself at all? One answer is obvious:

the lessons of history demonstrate that business has no choice. It must enlarge the range of its activities in the interest of its own long-range survival as one of the main supports of a free society. The alternative is a progressive surrender of the nation's business to political control and the further loss of scope in management.

To cope with environmental, conservational, and other problems will require philosophic wisdom as well as economic understanding. The adjustments involved will present a hazard to efficiency and stability. They will cut into the traditional motivations and incentives of businessmen. To understand the adjustments, business will need wise participants with diverse points of view to help make its decisions. Solutions to environmental problems, for example, even now require that competition be commingled with collaboration within and among business organizations, as well as between business and governmental agencies.

Modifying Administrative Structure

Where should these newly emerging responsibilities be assigned in the pyramidal organization tied to maximum efficiency and minimum unit costs? There is no comfortable fit. The evident answer is that additional organizational devices are required, devices that supplement the present relationships among the traditional line and staff functions.

One obvious device is to make social considerations a major input, along with economic factors, in the discussions prior to the drafting of the annual operating budget. The directional development of the corporation, embodied in its five- or ten-year strategic plans, provides another opportunity to appraise methodically shifts in public attitudes and to evaluate their impact on resource allocation and internal administrative policies. The periodic distribution to the organization of annual operating budgets and of longer-period strategic plans, incorporating the background thinking and assumptions that went into their preparation, can be helpful in awakening an awareness of social issues throughout an organization. But there remains the difficult task of reconciling the traditional incentives and motivations at the working levels with responses to the dual economic and social influences.

If the corporation is to be effective in its new and strange world, responsibilities must be assigned in ways that are now novel and unfamiliar. Traditional corporate units alone cannot cope with the tasks. To be sure, the traditional pyramidal structure has neat and understandable orderliness. By successive downward delegations of responsibility, authority, and accountability, business assignments get done. There is, however, a continuous centripetal pressure to push decisions inward to the center. That is especially true with regard to anything new or novel.

Even though annual operating budgets and longer-term strategic plans may have been developed to incorporate social as well as economic matters, and their terms have become well known throughout the organization, long-established habits will make difficult their effective translation into operating programs. The opportunity to better the financial projections of the budget plans by the neglect of costly societal actions will be hard to resist. Moreover, occasional variations in the respective points of view of staff and line officers further complicate the adjustments that will be required. Staff divisions, in contrast to line, ostensibly serve as expert counselors in their respective areas of expertise. But, lurking beneath the professed teamwork of line and staff divisions is an inherent ambiguity in the two channels of authority in the decision process. A built-in competitive conflict surfaces occasionally as to how limited resources will be used.

Traditional line and staff hierarchies, despite their familiar

112

relationships, are finding it harder to reach decisions as both business and societal problems become more complex. This is especially true if a department head feels responsible to two or more senior men. The practice is now evolving of creating, out of line and staff personnel, task groups to expedite decisions on specific problems. The chairman of such an ad hoc group must be skilled in working with diverse personalities and talents. The whole process, now sometimes called "matrix management," sometimes "project management," is designed to achieve the flexibility and capability for action of a small company by giving visibility to the potentials for conflict. Matrix or project management, it should be noted, is more collaborative than competitive.

Nor is the *research* or *study* task force new to the corporation as a collaboration of diverse skills, assigned to project-oriented problems. It has been used for many years. It has been assigned to special projects, or for the introduction of new methods, often on a temporary basis. Yet it need not be temporary. Some corporations have permanent units that act as internal agencies offering multiple services to associated departments. These groups are generally brought together out of the line and staff personnel. And they may include, and, in certain cases, probably should include, outside participants.

Of course, many day-to-day business operations have societal aspects: closing a plant or expanding one in an already crowded community; energy conservation in all phases of a company's activities; the training and best use of new entrants to the labor force from the female or minority population; the introduction of new processes or new product technology. Still other ongoing problems have induced corporations to supplement the traditional administrative structures. Separate departments have been established to design and develop pollution control equipment, to follow regulatory affairs pertaining to pollution and conservation, to test operations on employee health and teach safe product handling, and to deal with solid waste disposal. But it is when the corporation moves outside its normal business functions that it exposes itself to major new risks. It is then that the greatest impact on structure occurs.

For example, there has been much discussion of business participation in raising the quality of life in the inner cities. Some of this has already begun to occur through the return of suburbanites to the urban center. A recent study of the Committee for Economic Development, however, called

> particularly on private industry, state and local governments, and citizens to explore means of identifying and implementing solutions to urban life.[9]

A corporate commitment to participate in urban rehabilitation raises the question of who will make the investment. Who will pay the operating bill? There are numerous alternatives to choose from. If an assignment is given to a newly organized action group within the company, it could operate either for the account of the corporation—which is the least likely—or as an agent of the government for a fee, or for a joint account with the government. The group involved would differ from the characteristic study or research group. Illustrative is the General Motors lead participation to refurbish, through a newly organized subsidiary, six blocks of a residential section of Detroit, financed one-third from private sources, with the rest from city, state, and federal funds. Another instance is the City Venture Corporation, formed by Control Data Corporation with a group of partners, to revive the core of depressed cities.

This kind of *action* unit has been known to business for some time. NASA, in its successful space program, subcontracted parts of its total activities to corporations. The earlier Manhattan Project, which developed the atomic bomb, was another dramatic example. During World War II, government corporations extensively used private corporations as commission agents to procure urgently needed foreign supplies. But the precedent of contracting out has not yet been used extensively to deal with the alleviation of social ills.[10]

Many would object that it would be diversionary for a business to participate in arrangements with, or contract with, government for the provision of public services to ameliorate social problems. But there appear to be growing pressures in the country today, to do so, as our democracy searches for its public will. Governmental agencies at all levels now provide public services of many kinds that require some 30 percent or more of the nation's GNP to finance. The public may soon put a tax ceiling on that part of the national product they are willing to shift from private to public hands. Contracting out would not necessarily change the end use of total funds between social and business purposes, but it would represent a shift of activity back to private hands, thus limiting the growth of government employment, which, rachet-like, never seems to shrink. There is also a conviction that the productivity of social services can be increased.

Some in the government no doubt dislike the very idea of a profit; and to have a business corporation make a profit on a contract as an agent for the government to provide public services or to alleviate social ills can be a sore point. Hostility among civil servants results as well from the competitive pressures placed on public agencies. But, it may be necessary to abandon such notions if the combining of government resources with business talents and incentives should prove to be the least costly way for the nation to accomplish the job of social reconstruction. And, if a massive program using corporations as agents of government should be mounted, it would compel a major restructuring of certain aspects of corporate administration.

This does not mean business organizations would rush to dissolve existing departments, but growing up alongside the traditional departments there would be new structures to accomplish new purposes. This can be very disturbing to managers who have lived only under the old and stable management habits. Such managers like to have things precise, orderly, and carefully worked out, with lines of authority clearly identified. Then one can relax with these smooth working arrangements, or so it is said. But it is not, and never has been, quite that way. Numerous *new* problems, both internal and external, in unending procession have been challenging the traditional habits. Contract work for governments will be another challenge.

The criteria for career progress must be extended to include more than a person's contribution to short-term financial results. Social criteria, hard but not impossible to measure, must be included. When an individual now is taken out of the accustomed line of career progression and out of the routine activities of the corporation, it is disquieting. One wonders what will happen to his or her career—will he or she get lost? Lines of authority become confused, and responsibilities must be clarified and reclarified. Those who have experimented with matrix or project management have found the transition is not easy. New working relationships and interpersonal skills must be developed, based more on consensus than authority.

These ambiguous new organizational forms require consensus and cooperation, the opposite of the traditional competition among personnel. Recall that the administrative pyramid was designed to be most effective in a competitive situation. In contrast, these task forces and action groups—if they are to be effective—must acquire an attitude of collaboration within themselves. It is not easy to measure the performance of individuals on a task force. In many cases even the success of the group itself can be measured only over an extended period of time. These are significant, but not insurmountable, difficulties. And they can be small as compared with the advantages of the flexibility, adaptability, and initiative that

116

such innovative organizational structure can generate. The paramount adjustment required to reconcile competitive efficiencies with social commitments will be the formation of working relationships between the pyramidal line and staff departments and these new "special task" groupings.

Experience analogous to participation in these new relationships has existed for a long time, for many traditional staff functions cut across line departments. Although it has not been easy, this reconciliation of staff and line has had the unifying advantage of an acceptance of the primacy of competition and the bottom line. Now the adjustment will be even more difficult, for the concept of collaboration will increasingly stand alongside competition as a motivation. It is evident, however, that if the corporation is to shift the focus of its purposes to encompass the dual roles of business efficiency and societal concerns, the basic changes must occur at the working level of the departments and project-assigned task forces.

In another set of activities, the interface between the corporation and government has begun to affect corporate structure. Numerous municipalities, as well as state and federal agencies, have on request received the temporary services of business executives on loan to apply corporate administrative and communications technology to governmental operations. Joint business-government task forces dealing with such diverse matters as purchasing methods, cash management, personnel practices, records management, budgeting, and construction have often made major contributions to improved public administration. Of course, the removal of key executives from corporate operations for varying periods of time is still another disturbing element in business operations as the corporation goes out into the community. And sometimes a whole company instead of an individual manager will be commissioned to survey a particular governmental problem or department; the results in dislocation of normal activities may be very much the same. But despite the problems to business as it involves itself more deeply in the improvement of what are essentially social or socioeconomic problems, business has no real alternative but to participate in those new challenges if society is to reject an all pervasive government, with all the restrictions on traditional liberties that that implies.

Notes

1. Kenneth R. Andrews, "Can the Best Corporations Be Made Moral?," *Harvard Business Review,* Vol. 51, No. 3, May–June, 1973, p. 61.

2. *First Chicago World Report,* Jan.-Feb. 1978.

3. *Time,* June 12, 1978.

4. *New York Times,* June 24, 1978.

5. Henry Kissinger, address published in *Future of Business* (The Center for Strategic and International Studies, Georgetown University, June, 1977), p. 9.

6. Theodore Hauser, *Big Business and Human Values* (1957), p. 23.

7. From the *Burson-Marsteller Report,* August 1978/No. 49.

8. *New York Times,* May 2, 1978, p. 53.

9. Committee for Economic Development, *Social Responsibility of Business Corporations: A Statement on National Policy by the Research and Policy Committee* (New York: June 1971).

10. A clarification of the right to do so in certain municipal services was rendered by the New York State Appeals Court in June 1978.

7

Business-Government
Relations

CHANGES in the larger affairs of mankind, like Carl Sandburg's fog, seem to walk on cat's feet and literally steal upon the observer. Such is the case with the myriad relationships between business and government in the United States, at municipal, state, and federal levels. It is true whether the relationship is regulatory, financial, collaborative, or advisory. And there has been an enormous increase in the number and frequency of contacts between government and business. At the same time, the nature of these contacts has gone beyond those concerned with identified fields of business. New relationships have resulted from comprehensive governmental interest in social as well as purely business matters. Some of these changes have been constructive; but by no means all. Far from it.

So similar are many aspects of government and business operations, if not decision making, that one often hears of the urgent need for more business knowledge in government and more government knowledge in business. Indeed, it is no isolated opinion that the leaders of business in years to come will be called on to assume many of the functions that historically have been exercised by politicians. Needless to say,

119

there is less enthusiasm among businessmen for politicians performing the tasks of business, yet a great deal of this has already occurred. This intermingling of functions has drifted in without much conscious thought given to its implications. In part, it is a derivative of the growing acceptance by business leaders of quality-of-life considerations alongside of economic factors in their decision making. In part, the substitution of political for private control of our complex economy reflects a lack of confidence in the ability of the pricing system to do its work of resource allocation.

When the business corporation was thought of as purely economic in nature, a discrete separation of functions between private business and government was rational. Private business existed to produce and sell goods and services. Its success would fill an ever-expanding cornucopia of material wealth in forms desired by the public, and it would increase the opportunities for self-fulfillment. The functions of the government were clear also. Government would set the ground rules by maintaining the validity of contract and a stable currency. It would provide defense against external aggression, use its police powers to enforce laws, describe the outer limits of permissible business practice, and monitor the business community to assure a free market and an open society.

Quality-of-life considerations have always been on the agenda of government concerns, but until recent decades, the value structure of the nation has placed self-reliance and individual initiative higher than consumer protection, welfare, and the maintenance by government of minimum standards of well-being. Likewise, quality-of-life considerations, while not totally neglected, have until recent decades been among the secondary considerations of business. As social matters have moved toward the center stage of national concern, business and government functions have so overlapped that it is now sometimes hard to say where government begins and business stops, or vice versa.

Yet some functions are still uniquely the province of governments. These concern matters in which governments are expected to take initiating action, just as business is expected to initiate action in other areas. Each has strengths less available or unavailable to the other. Thus, there is the taxing, coinage, and police power of government, on the one hand, and the productive, marketing, and innovative risk-taking activities of business, on the other hand. In between, there is a penumbra of purposes and activities, most of which are related to quality-of-life considerations, where the comparative strengths of government and business are less identifiable. It is in this area of overlap that the major opportunities exist for business-government collaboration.

Unfortunately, the pattern of business-government relations today bears little relevance to the respective strengths of the two: instead of a mixed economy, we have a mixed-up economy! It is a sad combination of distrust of business by government officials, a low appraisal of the abilities of government personnel by businessmen, and a public confusion about both that is acquired through the mass media. But an appraisal of the areas of comparative strengths can disclose opportunities for both government and business to improve their performances.

The Work of Government

Regulation, supported by the police power, is an area in which governments—federal, state, and municipal—have primary strength. An elaboration of the endless accumulation of detailed federal regulation of business is redundant, for the story has been told many times. The situation is grave, to say the least; even elected officials are, at last, beginning to condemn the encroachments. The most socially and politically destructive assumption is the belief that administrative decisions can obtain a result more compatible with the public interest than one obtained by the free choice of many individuals in the open market. There is little or no interest among government regulators in the market's ability to allocate resources. Witness the complex proposals for a national energy policy, and the protective devices that have been designed to cushion domestic interests from foreign competition. Witness the minimum wage increase in an inflationary period, and the increases in farm price supports. One could go on: more and more regulatory restraint on business, intervention by government, and the nonstop growth of the bureaucracy.

Underpinning these national programs is the notion, strongly held by many government officials and only less so by those sectors of business directly affected, that market solutions are bound to be unfair. The fact is that the burdens are simply shifted to the public at large by the expanding involvement of government, higher taxes, higher prices, and retarded economic growth. For example, while only a handful of the public accepts the desirability of a no-growth economy, the widely endorsed goals of antipollution and conservation, and the discouragement of the development of some forms of energy, are combining to constrain the once clear priority for growth. In other words, it is not simply a matter of distrust of the businessman by the government bureaucracy; it is a distrust of the economic system to which the businessman is allegedly dedicated.

In turn, the businessman strongly disdains the typical behavior of the government official who supports obedience to the established rules and respect for the vested interests of the hierarchy, irrespective of particular circumstances. Adaptation and flexibility are incompatible with closely structured regulations. Some regulation is essential to set the "ground rules," and maintain orderliness and stability. There is a strong conviction, however, that federal regulatory practices have gone beyond the point of optimum utility. The states, with their newly acquired jurisdiction in antitrust matters, and the municipalities, worried about overcrowding, are not far behind in the regulatory activities. A really significant contraction of this debilitating process of over-regulation will require prior improvement of public confidence in business and a more convincing rationale than has yet been presented. A tough struggle indeed!

Consumer protection has come to be taken as one of the basic justifications for the enormous expansion of economic regulation. When the issues are safety in the plant, security in careers and retirement, or product integrity and warranties, the public has accepted the notion that self-regulation is inadequate. Yet when all the regulatory red tape is combined and measured, the end result is probably counterproductive, and economically choking. Better that self-regulation were made more convincing and effective. This is seen clearly in the light of the basic changes taking place in the competitive global economy. Numerous lesser-developed countries, such as Mexico, Taiwan, South Korea, Singapore, and Brazil, have substantially expanded their industrial capacity. Unit costs of production are typically lower than those of the older industrialized nations—such as the United States, Western Europe, and even Japan—in all of which these same pressures exist for massive subsidies to sustain uneconomic industries in global competition. Those subsidies are paid directly out of the public purse—which means out of individual pocketbooks.

Another area in which government has unique initiating strength, and an area in desperate need of attention, is the maintenance of the stability of the currency and of the design of incentives to accumulate and invest capital. Both have been seriously damaged by government actions and inactions in recent decades. The inflation that has persisted at varying rates since World War II will ultimately destroy civil and political liberties, as well as economic abundance and freedoms, unless it is first contained and then eliminated. The record of recent years is ominous. From 1947 to 1965, inflation averaged 2.5 percent a year; from 1966 to 1971, it averaged 4.5 percent; from 1972 to 1978, it reached 7.7 percent. Now there is a fear that the rate may continue at a double-digit level.

Long since forgotten is the thought that *no* inflation—not less inflation—will most equitably serve all the people. Improvements in productivity could then be passed on to all consumers, as they were during most of the nineteenth century, by means of lower unit costs of production and corresponding price declines. That is a situation that has precedence; prices in the nation tended to drift downward for one hundred years; they were lower in 1900 than in 1800.

Among the most significant benefits of the termination of governmentally induced inflation would be a lessening of group pressures to acquirement through the exercise of political muscle. Something was said in Chapter 4 of this book of the debilitating effects of inflation, rising taxes, and regulation on the maintenance or enlargement of capital formation. Without revision of the government's inflationary policies, the expectations of slower national growth are certain to be realized. Job expansion and career development will go begging. Tension and discontent will mount, and business will not go blameless. Its leadership must exercise a restraining influence in numerous ways, including its own self-discipline.

The Work of Business

Business really has no alternative to bringing these threatening issues forcefully to the awareness of the public and through the public to the attention of our politicians. That is no easy assignment, for businessmen have a distaste for politics. Moreover, a case must be made that seeks the national interest—not the interest of any one industry or corporation. The case must have clarity and integrity. Inflation *is* pernicious. Its devastation is most ominous in its threat to the open market, and an impairment of the open market, in the long run, represents an erosion of the commitment to political democracy.

No business concern has more urgency than giving voice to the unbalanced cost-benefit results of inflationary and regulatory policies. As business corporations are now structured, they are poorly equipped to offer that kind of guidance. The policies related to inflation and regulation are the jurisdiction of government. Only government can modify them. Business can influence change only if the deeply held public conviction can be *removed* that business speaks first for its own interest and secondarily for the public. The sustained inflation of recent decades is, in a real sense, an imposition of taxes, in part imposed on the impoverished but also on productive capital. It has resulted in an indiscriminate shift in the allocation of resources that undermines the strength of the economy, the level of total activity, and the opportunity for expanded employment.

Too often in the past, business has found a little inflation —not too much—quite agreeable. Regulation also has been selectively approved—and disapproved. Seldom is an objection made to taxes on a particular activity if a part of the government receipts are used directly or indirectly to subsidize that particular activity. All such self-serving positions undermine credibility.

The development of effective self-regulation, industry by industry, could have avoided much externally imposed control. In that case, it would have been carried out with a higher degree of knowledge and sophistication, and probably would have avoided a part of the incremental increases in unit costs of production. It may still be possible here to "turn back the clock" by the development of self-regulation to replace some of the present rigid and ineffective regulatory procedures. But this new day can dawn only through the initiative of business in collaboration with enlightened government leadership. The effort is sure to be resisted by the bureaucracy of government. It will require tenaciously sustained effort by business to win public approval.

Joint Assignments

Government and business come face to face on other fronts. Governments are among the largest customers of business, although the amount of government business on the books of business corporations varies from time to time, company to company, and field to field. Those supplying military equipment do so much of their business with the federal government that it is difficult still to catalogue them as private organizations, even though technically owned by stockholders. The assurance of sources of supply has induced governments to provide subsidized and high-risk financing to keep such corporations afloat. In these cases, it is hard to know whether the policies and the foreign and domestic contacts of the organization are privately or publicly determined—take Lockheed as an example. But government as a major customer is not confined to military items by any means. When the protesting students of the late 1960s tried to target those corporations contributing supplies to the Vietnam War, they found it difficult to find any that were not. This customer-supplier relationship between government and business has created a continuous, expanding channel of familiarity for closer collaboration in other types of contacts.

And businessmen more than ever are serving as part-time, or even full-time, consultants to government. The nagging difficulties of New York City furnish an interesting example of the consultative capabilities of business. For many years organizations of businessmen have studied the population, employment, commercial, cultural, and financial trends of the "Big Apple" and have made periodic reports of their findings. When the financial affairs of the city reached a crisis, both the city and state governments turned to the business community for the talent and imagination to retrieve the situation. Advisors and consultants from business became designers of programs and procedures, yes, and even negotiators. New York City has not been unique in this kind of arrangement. Without the smoke of crises, many communities, cities, counties, and states, have enlisted and encouraged experienced organizations of business talent to assist in a wide variety of efforts to improve public administration.

Another government-business connection has grown rapidly: formal joint ventures, or less formal partnerships, to coordinate their respective strengths in specific programs. These have occurred at the municipal level as well as at the state and federal. The strengths of the corporation are several: long experience in finding efficient means to do a job, people to do it, adaptability to different tasks, and a strong inventory of technology. The federal government has enlisted these strengths in building the atomic bomb, in nuclear fuel enrichment and reprocessing, in the effort to find new sources of energy, in global communications, and conspicuously in the program to put a man on the moon. Local government has found redevelopment of the center city to be extraordinarily complex and has sought to coordinate its efforts in a partnership with business, if not in a formally organized joint venture. Mass transit, parking, sewage, crime control, and tax provisions must be synchronized with financing, zoning variances, design, and construction. In most federal and local programs that draw private sector participa-

127

tion, it has been discovered that a simplification of governmental procedures can expedite the work.

The field of transportation is noteworthy as one in which business and government have used each other's strengths. The building of the interstate highways, the nation's waterways, and port facilities, the takeover of most of the nation's railroad passenger business and part of the freight—all have resulted in public services that would have been beyond the capability of private business without making unacceptable charges. On the other hand, evidence has accumulated that the operation of businesses by government, including transportation, typically leads to deterioration of the service.

It is plausible to expect that by combining the respective strengths of government and business—especially in the area of quality-of-life considerations—an optimum resolution could be made of some of the seemingly intractable complexities. It is not valid to think of the issue in terms of governmental ownership or control versus private property and free enterprise. As Frederick Lewis Allen observed a quarter of a century ago, the ideologies of pure socialism and pure capitalism are both passé. The United States has long since passed beyond either of them to a more sophisticated sociopolitical economy that blends some of the most pertinent elements of each.

The corporation is in the midstream of adjustment to a social and political order that is accommodating the community's concern for the values of humanism with a tenacious commitment to the excellence inherited from the age of reason. It is not a matter of history returning full circle to the seventeenth and eighteenth centuries, when the corporation was essentially an arm of government to serve what was conceived to be the national interest. But, it is to be hoped, more opportunities will be found to join government and business in the public interest. The adversary relationship between them should then diminish, maybe vanish.

As former President Clarence C. Walton of Catholic University observed in commenting on an essay by Professor George Cabot Lodge:

Adjusting to the emerging ideology may be as painful to contempories as adjustment to the liberal economy was painful to committed mercantilists of the eighteenth century. But adjustments must be made because the philosophical tide is irreversible: we shall ride it out or we shall be engulfed. Since the State is destined to play a greater role, accommodation to this development may indeed be one of the most painful adjustments that corporate executives will have to make.[1]

Note

1. Clarence C. Walton, *The Ethics of Corporate Conduct* (Englewood Cliffs: Prentice-Hall, 1978), p. 79.

8

Innovation Abroad

The growth of international trade, international investment, international licensing, multinational enterprises, and international banking has produced a new economic structure, accompanied by marked increases in overall efficiency. . . . Today with upwards of $350 billion of assets held by Americans in foreign countries and $275 billion or so held by foreigners in the United States, we are irretrievably linked to the world economy.[1]

Most of these interchanges of capital, products, and services have taken place since World War II, and most have taken place through the activities of business corporations. The difficult transition experienced by domestic corporations from the single goal of profit-making to the multiple purposes of profits *and* wider participation in society becomes even more complicated when recognition must be accorded the often conflicting political purposes and differing cultures of other nations. As a result, multinational corporations have been the target of much defamatory attention, even more than domestic companies.

These attacks are not without precedent. Despite the role the multinational corporation has played for centuries in the development of the world of nation-states, it has never been conspicuously popular, either at home or abroad. The Russia Company, the Levant Company, and the East India Company, all chartered in England in the sixteenth century to find export markets for woolens and other British products, also found it profitable to export from their foreign outposts and sell in third country markets in competition with the home country. Imports into Britain were especially unwelcome. This, of course, frustrated the basic mercantile purpose of acquiring, through favorable trade balances, larger stocks of gold and silver for the home country. Later the Virginia Company and the Plymouth Company were chartered to colonize the New World, but their overseas production, it was held, in the colonies or in third countries was not supposed to compete with that of the home country. In other words, the early multinational companies were chartered to serve the interests of the home country, and that they did even though they were criticized. England, Holland, France, and Portugal, all with chartered companies, expanded and developed into strong world powers. Spain's influence, without chartered companies, did not last as long.

The notion lingers to this day that a multinational company should and will serve primarily the interests of its home country nationals and the home country government. Foreign-owned companies are inherently suspect by the people and governments of host countries. For example, witness the attitudes and concerns currently felt and expressed by the citizens of the United States at the encroachment of foreign owners in this nation's banks.

Criticism of the multinational company takes numerous forms. Host governments, finding it difficult to keep closely informed about the multinational corporations of other nations within their borders, feel concern that these foreign corporations may at times serve as convenient agents for their home governments' pursuit of purposes incompatible with local policies. The assumption by governments, since the Great Depression, of major influence on internal economic affairs, implies a degree of economic nationalism. Transfer payments among corporate components of a multinational company, it is felt, provide the opportunity for artificial pricing and tax evasion. Even efficiency is often resented. Crushing or buying out local competition is sometimes alleged. Market prices may be fixed, and competitive behavior constrained by the host government. Accusations are made that local labor is exploited. Constituencies of home governments, on the other hand, complain that jobs are exported, that domestic productive capability is diminished, and that the economy is weakened. Yet, despite the crescendo of concern in both home and host countries, international investment and international trade in recent decades have grown at a more rapid rate than domestic investment and internal trade. The large corporation that has *not* acquired interests in other countries is now more the exception than the rule.

The Spread of Global Investment

At a faster pace than many realize, great manufacturing and trading companies have developed a vast interwoven network of communications and interests, of procedures for the transfer of technology and commercial intelligence, and of personnel that cuts across national boundaries and cultural patterns. Unlike the situation that obtains in a political settlement, global companies operate in a context in which their negotiations do not carry a heavy baggage of emotional commitment, and in which a resolution of a problem can be beneficial to both parties. They provide a network of interconnected conduits that facilitate the optimum utilization of financial, material, and technical resources. As a unifying influence, the multinational companies are a powerful force in the world today. Concomitantly, they provide an equilibrating tendency in the global economy, when they are able to place their production where it can achieve the lowest unit cost and sell where the returns are highest. "Business has an immense future," in the opinion of Henry Kissinger, "of opportunity and responsibility, in helping to meet the development challenge." [2]

These optimistic thoughts, however, must necessarily be accompanied by the realization that managing the multinational corporation is highly complex. The task of appraising a rapidly changing world economic order to achieve maximum efficiency and return on investment is a highly sophisticated exercise. In addition, adaptation must be made to differing social expectations in numerous cultures and to the often conflicting and overlapping political positions of competing national governments.

A succinct recitation of several of the major trends in world business will serve to demonstrate the risks as well as the opportunities for the business corporation operating on a global scale. In combination, the several basic changes now occurring, in the opinion of close observers, will result in a modified structure of world business that will differ markedly from the past. The United States has lost some of its lead in productivity and technology, first to Western Europe and Japan, and then surprisingly to the "advanced developing countries": Brazil and Mexico in South and Central America, and to Korea, Taiwan, Singapore, and Hong Kong in the Far East. As the cost of energy increases relative to the cost of labor, the comparative advantage of the developing countries will be further enhanced, especially relative to Western Europe and Japan, which are heavily dependent on external sources of energy.

Adjusting to the World Economy

The rate of economic growth in the less-developed countries has been greater than that in the developed countries, and since most of them are in the Southern Hemisphere, a shift of industrial production toward the South is occurring. Access to raw materials supports the shift. Food production, however, has lagged in the less-developed world. The availability of land to produce cereals, grasses, and forest products is diminishing relative to the growth of global population. Forward strides have been made in technology for fishing and mining the seas, but the political issues of entitlement are far from resolved. The raw materials of mines are scarcer and the real costs of their extraction are rising. The limits of the earth's energy reserves of liquid and gaseous hydrocarbons have become a matter of global concern. Though needed by all nations, their availability and cost are tied to the decisions of the OPEC nations.

All of these matters are basic to the rate of world economic growth and to the trade and investment relationships among nations and regions to each other. They imply a slower rate of total global growth, and a gradual "closing of the gap" of the less-developed world, together with a further political assertiveness on the part of the less-developed countries. The emerging structure of the world economy will make difficult the maintenance of nondiscriminatory and liberal trade and investment policies. Indeed, as *Business Week* magazine has observed:

> In a world . . . where the established countries are threatened by intensified competition from the lesser developed countries, regaining the momentum toward freer trade would require superhuman statesmanship.[3]

The experience of recent years has resulted in a loss of confidence that governments can manage their internal economic affairs without isolating outside influences. The persistence of inflation, in combination with unemployment and a slowing rate of economic growth, has resulted in inward-looking policies, especially in the developed world. Quotas, nontariff barriers, and "orderly marketing" agreements are much in evidence. A common currency has been proposed for Western Europe, in part to protect against the declining value of the U.S. dollar. The tentative efforts of Europe, Japan, and the United States to carve out their own spheres of economic influence could result in the development of a regionalism, within each of which a reasonable degree of nondiscriminatory trade and investment could occur.

In this highly complex world economy, the multinational corporation may be the major remaining force for economic integration. But its managers must be aware that any form of integration necessarily qualifies a nation's ability to be wholly independent. Interdependence involves adjustment costs and as a major integrating agent, the multinational corporation cannot wholly avoid ruffling the sensitivities of foreign governments, especially in the less-developed world.

Adjusting to World Cultures and Politics

Adaptation to a rapidly changing world economy is one thing; adaptation to the aspirations and cultural patterns of local population and to the political policies of local governments is another. Personnel practices in different parts of the world are a crucial area that requires adaptability and adjustment to cultural differences and change. To pay wages comparable with those of the home country would require the establishment of compounds to keep the nonbeneficiaries out—hardly a desirable solution. Yet to pay wages comparable with those in the host country exposes a business to accusations of exploitation by labor leaders at home. And personnel practices differ widely among countries—from

Japan, to France, to the Latin American countries. The impact of demographic trends will differ markedly from those of the United States. Population, especially in the less-developed countries, is increasing so rapidly, it is expected that, on a global basis, the reserve army of the unemployed will reach alarming totals in a few years. It has been estimated that by 1995, or in less than twenty years, the total world labor force seeking employment may grow by a billion people from just over 1.6 billion to nearly 2.6 billion.[4] This, coupled with increasing evidence of slower global economic growth, could spell social and political instability.

In political matters, the multilateral corporation must adapt to more than one national jurisdiction. Apart from the effort of the U.S. government to impose rules on foreign affiliates through extraterritorial application of U.S. laws—antitrust for example—there have been numerous cases in which enforcement of foreign political policy has, in the past, been attempted by using multinational companies: proscribing the shipment, by a U.S. subsidiary, of Canadian wheat to China or truck parts to Cuba. Each nation-state thinks of itself as an important economic actor in its own domestic and foreign affairs, responding to the perceived political needs of its citizens. The opportunity is always present to develop adversary relationships with the quite different objectives of the multinational corporation. Yet accommodation has been and must continue to be made. Whether willing or not, the managers of multinational corporations are being forced to accept some of the conflicting pressures of world politics.

An interesting contrast in cultural attitudes is provided by recent U.S. legislation proscribing foreign payments (to obtain contract business) on penalty of severe liability. Some have interpreted this as an attempt to impose American morality on the traditional practices of other people. The

136

New York Times recently quoted a British businessman in Hong Kong with the cynical remark:

"Who are the Americans to tell us about morality? What's business all about anyway—to make money. You pay a commission to make a deal, you make a profit, everybody's happy."

And the British can write-off such a payment on their tax returns as a necessary business expense.

Managerial Innovation

The Greek god Proteus was hard to get a hold on; when seized or cornered, he disengaged himself simply by changing shape. It is in the sense of a supple innovator that the modern corporation has proven a worldly inheritor of the protean tradition. Its capacity to adapt its structure, procedures, and commitments to the requirements of evolving circumstances has confounded its critics, while delighting its supporters. Cast in the role of world developer, yet hemmed in by a wide array of cultural, political, financial, and even military obstacles, it has had to pioneer or pull out. The withdrawal of IBM from India is a conspicuous example of the latter, and it should be noted that the number of smaller divestments has tended to increase in recent years. But, for the most part, the multinational corporation has elected to stay and pioneer—in ways that some would have thought unworkable, radical, or simply absurd a half-century ago.

The earliest modification of traditional direct foreign investment was the joint venture, in which equity ownership is shared in varying proportions with citizens of the receiving countries or with the host government. In the area of natural resource industries—oil and minerals—imaginative modifications of the joint venture, including novel self-liquidating financial arrangements, have been developed to give recognition to both the home country's inherent property rights and the contributions of capital and capability of foreign enterprises.

A nonequity form of joint venture is the service contract under which the "investing" company agrees with a host representative—again either the government or private groups—to provide services for a fixed fee. When the "service" includes the creation and management of a previously nonexistent enterprise, the arrangement goes by the name of a "management contract." A variant of the management contract, the "co-production scheme," is used in Soviet-bloc countries. The private business in this setup may supply machinery, technology, management, and perhaps a market, with the host government furnishing the plant, workers, and the raw materials. Compensation for the foreign partner may be by fee or, more typically, by a predetermined share of the end product.

All of these arrangements are supplementary to the more traditional form of foreign investment: the overseas affiliate that holds indefinite tenure of title in the country of operation. Whether these practices represent transitional steps, in the development of regional or global arrangements, which will in turn diminish their necessity or desirability is a question that cannot now be answered. It is sufficient to say that, in the aggregate, they represent a significant enlargement of the capability of the modern corporation to adapt itself to a world of cultural, economic, and political disparities.

The imaginative means by which the multinational corporation has spread its commitments around the globe are an interesting part—but only a part—of the story. The complexities associated with its daily operation require comparable initiatives, adaptability, and sensitivity.

A variety of trade policies and practices have developed throughout the world regarding monopoly and competition. Adaptations to the competitive practices of a host country may, and frequently do, run afoul of the antitrust position of the United States; yet competitive disadvantages with local firms may be incurred through failure to adapt. The participation of a Gulf Oil affiliate in a Canadian government sponsored uranium cartel was a dramatic example. A host of financial problems with novel features emerges in the acquisition of new capital in foreign markets, the transfer of funds, and even in the wide variety of accounting requirements and practices in different countries. Indeed, intracompany transactions become international transactions.

New concepts of organizational structure and management control have been designed. Personnel policies for both management and labor, adjusted to personal needs as well as local custom and legislation, have been developed. Clearly there is no shortage of problems ahead for the worldwide business organization. Despite its newness as a major world influence and its vast reservoir of unsolved problems, it is pregnant with great promise. The demands and problems that will shape the multinational corporation of tomorrow relate more to political versus business values than to those of humanism versus materialism; and the impact of political influences will remain as an inextricable conditioner of their policies and practices.

A lesson can be learned from the experience of the foreign affiliates of global organizations. Whether their home base is in the United States, Europe, Japan, Latin America, or even Southeast Asia, these foreign affiliates have had to make adjustments imposed by economic, cultural, and political circumstances. It is heartening to see how flexible and perceptive business has been in its response to newly encountered circumstances. Now an additional pressure is beginning to make itself felt throughout the global business world with the recrudescence in public thinking of post-industrial concern for the individual. It will take many years for this emerging influence to be felt in a dominant manner in the less-developed world, but even there it is not without present influence.

The reconciliation of the values of science, which did so much to develop the modern business corporation, with those of the humanism now being reasserted, has caused much confusion in managing the purely domestic corporation. But that does not mean that no progress is evident either at home or abroad. A growing awareness of the values of humanism blended with those of rationalism will be a powerful influence in helping both the multinational and the purely domestic corporation to achieve productive destinies.

Notes

1. W. Michael Blumenthal, *Foreign Affairs*, July 1978, pp. 728–739.

2. Henry Kissinger, address, published in *Future of Business* (The Center for Strategic and International Studies, Georgetown University, June, 1977), p. 14.

3. *Business Week*.

4. "Population," The Population Crisis Committee, Washington, D.C., September, 1977, No. 7.

9

Description:
Preface to Prescription

COMMENTING on his decision not to run for reelection, Massachusetts Democrat Michael J. Harrington was quoted in the *Wall Street Journal* of September 21, 1978:

> I'm optimistic by nature. I believe problems can be solved. But I'm not sanguine at this point that we even know what the problems are. We've got a lot of guys in Congress now who have mastered those techniques that will keep them in office. But how many can offer you a coherent sense of the whole? How many would even try?

This book is not about politics and legislative office holders. It is about the business corporation and its leaders, but Mr. Harrington's observation has relevance. The corporation also has problems, problems of credibility, even of legitimacy. An attempt has been made here to ferret out the essential nature of the overriding problem that must be recognized and ultimately resolved before business is restored to full public endorsement. Description and identification of the deep-rooted public pressures at work has been the focus more than a precise prescription for tomorrow's corporation. The latter can come only after the processes of trial and error, and the educational experiences that accompany them, have clarified the structures and practices that will best serve the public.

A number of apparent issues, which have dominated public debate in the media and in the business community about the business corporation and its activities, were discussed in Chapter 3. But the heart of the difficulty for business goes much deeper; it goes beyond the matters that provide the agenda of public debate. The central issue is the urgent need to find, within the purposes, administrative structures, and functioning of the corporation, a workable reconciliation between two powerful and contradictory sets of social values: humanism and materialism, the whole man and economic man. The social values of compassion, collective group action, collaboration, consensus, and conservation are now challenging the antithetical values on which the corporation has for two or more centuries built its great strength: the natural laws of science, individualism and self-reliance, the rewards and penalties of competition, authority based on hierarchy, and the aggressive exploitation of nature.

Adaptation to the emerging environment is no easy task for business managers, trained as they are in pursuing a single purpose, the efficiency that assures a maximum return on stockholders' investment. In doing so, business managers have had extraordinary success. The result is an abundance unimagined by earlier generations. Indeed, it is an abundance that has encouraged and made possible the resurgence of the values of humanism expressed as solicitude for the whole person. An approach to material satiation among a growing proportion of the population has removed some of the alarm from a possible diminution in the rate of economic growth.

The corporation as a centrally important institution of society has made another contribution of even greater importance, though it is less well recognized. It has made possible a highly complex, technologically based society, without resort to the all-enveloping direction of the political state. Without the business corporation, the state in an advanced society must necessarily appropriate the functions of the open market in the task of marshalling large resources, allocating their use, assigning employment, and determining the level and relationship of a wide range of prices.

Experience has shown convincingly that where this has occurred it has been accompanied by political repression. The corporation's silent defense of political democracy, almost by virtue of its existence, has been more significant than the hortatory free enterprise proclamations of its leaders. It is urgently important that the corporation be preserved in its full vigor in the interest of all the people— not just for those who own and manage it. The dilemma of corporate management is not found in what the corporation may ultimately become—it is in the discomfort of the process of change and the underlying nudging compulsions to choose among unfamiliar and often displeasing alternatives.

Acceptance of a multiplicity of corporate purposes carries with it numerous consequences, some of which are little understood and yet to be tested. Thus the traditional power structure of the corporation is designed to achieve only a maximum return on investment through ever greater efficiency and growth. This required a tight authoritative control of the corporation, and was expressed so well by a business leader of a generation ago, Clarence Randall, who said, "One man decides—the will of one man is the activating force—he speaks and others obey." A broadened range of purposes will, and indeed already has, required a modification of this authoritarian principle. Unquestioned authority in the corporation has given ground to an increase in collaboration and consensual decision making.

The assignments and functions respectively of executive management and members of the board of directors are beginning to reflect these new demands on the corporation. Organizational structures for administration have been designed to supplement the traditional line and staff pyramids that have been so effective in the singular pursuit of the bottom line. But constructive revision of the interface between government and business has yet to develop in a significant manner. Sorely needed is an altered attitude that would identify and use the relative strengths of each in a manner to maximize benefits in the response to public needs.

The business corporation is a truly remarkable social invention whose accomplishments in the past have been impressive, but whose opportunities for constructive good have only begun to be realized. A greater awareness of this fact by business management, by government personnel, and by the public at large would make its passage from a single to a multiple purpose organization less alarming and painful, and, indeed, more rational. A broad vision of the nature and direction of this evolution, accompanied by continued trial and error, provides a better assurance of service to the public than the detailed prescriptions of regulations.

The question noted in the first chapter of this book (Does the corporation have a future?) can be answered with a confident affirmation, but its future will be unlike its past. Other than that, the precise form and characteristics of its future are yet to be determined. It will be shaped more by the dominant values of the society that gives it sanction, as those values change through time, than by the conscious direction of its leaders. The optimum policies for corporate management will be to assure a sensitive response to changing public aspirations, and at the same time, preserve to the greatest extent possible, the great strengths of efficiency and capacity it now enjoys. Beyond the admonition of flexibility and adaptability, a detailed blueprint prescribing its future is of doubtful merit.

The business corporation's past contributions to material abundance have been notable. By means of its evolutionary development, it now has the great challenge of a complementary and equally auspicious career to enhance its service to the welfare of the human race.

Bibliography

ALLEN, FREDERICK LEWIS. *The Big Change*. New York: Harper & Row Publishers, Inc., 1952.

American Telephone & Telegraph Company. *Business and Society in Change*. 1975.

ANSHEN, MELVIN L. *Managing the Socially Responsible Corporation: the 1972–1973 Paul Garrett Lectures*. New York: Macmillan Publishing Co., Inc., 1974.

BAUMOL, WILLIAM J. "Business Responsibility and Economic Behavior." In *Managing the Socially Responsible Corporation*. Edited by Melvin Anshen. New York: Macmillan Publishing Co., Inc., 1974.

BERLE, A. A., JR. *The 20th Century Capitalist Revolution*. New York: Harcourt Brace & World, 1954.

BOULDING, KENNETH. *The Organizational Revolution: A Study in the Ethics of Economic Organization*. New York: Harper & Row Publishers, Inc., 1953.

BORK, ROBERT H. *The Antitrust Paradox: A Policy at War with Itself*. New York: Basic Books, 1978.

BROWN, COURTNEY C. *Putting the Corporate Board to Work*. New York: Macmillan Publishing Co., Inc., 1976.

CHAMBERLAIN, NEIL W. *The Limits of Corporate Responsibility*. New York: Basic Books, 1973.

CHILDS, MARGUIS; and CATER, DOUGLASS. *Ethics in a Business Society*. New York: Harper & Row, Publishers, Inc., 1954.

Committee for Economic Development. *Social Responsibility of Business Corporations: a Statement on National Policy by the Research and Policy Committee*. New York: June 1971.

DILL, WILLIAM R., ed. *Running the American Corporation*. New

York: The American Assembly, Columbia University, 1978 (unpublished workbook).

DRUCKER, PETER F. *The Concept of the Corporation*, 1946. New York: John Day Co., 1972, with a new preface and an epilogue.

DRUCKER, PETER F. *The New Society: The Anatomy of the Industrial Order*. New York: Harper, 1950.

EELLS, RICHARD. *Global Corporations: The Emerging System of World Economic Power*. New York: Interbook, Inc., 1972.

EELLS, RICHARD. *The Government of Corporations*. New York: Free Press of Glencoe, 1962.

GALBRAITH, JOHN KENNETH. *Economics and the Public Purpose*. Boston: Houghton Mifflin Co., 1973.

JACOBY, NEIL H. *Corporate Power and Social Responsibility*. New York: Macmillan, 1972.

KAHN, HERMAN; BROWN, WILLIAM; and MARTEL, LEON. *The Next 200 Years: A Scenario for America and the World*. New York: William Morrow & Co., Inc., 1976.

KAPLAN, ABRAHAM D. H. *Big Enterprise in a Competitive System*. Washington, D.C.: Brookings Institution, 1954.

KAYSEN, CARL; and TURNER, DONALD F. *Antitrust Policy: An Economic and Legal Analysis*. Cambridge, Mass.: Harvard University Press, 1965.

KUHN, JAMES W.; and BERG, IVAR. *Values in a Business Society: Issues and Analyses*. New York: Harcourt Brace Jovanovich, 1968.

LARSON, JOHN A., ed. *The Responsible Businessman: Business and Society*. (Readings from *Fortune*). New York: Holt, Rhinehart & Winston, 1966.

LIPPMANN, WALTER. *The Public Philosophy*. Boston: Little Brown & Co., 1955.

LOUDEN, J. KEITH. *The Effective Director in Action*. New York: American Management Association, 1975.

McKIE, JAMES, ed. *Social Responsibility and the Business Predicament*. Washington: Brookings Institution, 1974.

MUELLER, ROBERT K. *New Directions for Directors: Behind the By-Laws*. Massachusetts: Lexington Books, 1978.

NADER, RALPH; GREEN, MARK; and SELIGMAN, JOEL. *Taming the Giant Corporation*. New York: W. W. Norton & Co., Inc., 1976.

PALUSZEK, JOHN L. *Will the Corporation Survive?* Reston, Virginia: Reston Publishing Co., Inc., 1977.

RANDALL, JOHN H. JR. *Making of the Modern Mind: A Survey of the Intellectual Background of the Present Age.* (rev. ed.). Cambridge, Mass.: Houghton Mifflin, 1954.

ROBINSON, JOAN. *The Economics of Imperfect Competition.* 2nd ed. London: Macmillan Publishing Co., Ltd., 1969.

SETHI, S. PRAKASH. *Up Against the Corporate Wall.* Englewood Cliffs, New Jersey: Prentice-Hall, Inc., 1971.

SILK, LEONARD; and VOGEL, DAVID. *Ethics and Profits.* New York: Simon & Schuster, 1976.

SIMON, WILLIAM E. *A Time for Truth.* New York: McGraw-Hill, Inc., 1978.

STONE, CHRISTOPHER. *Where the Law Ends: The Social Control of Corporate Behavior.* New York: Harper & Row, 1976.

WALTON, CLARENCE C., ed. *Business and Social Progress.* New York: Praeger Publishers, 1970.

WALTON, CLARENCE C. *Corporate Social Responsibilities.* California: Wadsworth Publishing Co., 1967.

WEBER, MAX. *The Protestant Ethic and the Spirit of Capitalism.* New York: Scribner, 1958.

WHYTE, WILLIAM H., JR.; and the editors of *Fortune. Is Anybody Listening? How and Why U.S. Business Fumbles when it Talks with Human Beings.* New York: Simon & Schuster, 1952.

WILKINS, MIRA. *The Maturing of Multinational Enterprise.* Cambridge, Mass.: Harvard University Press, 1947.

Magazine Articles, Pamphlets, Readings, Forms, Reports, Speeches, and Others

BACON, JEREMY. *Corporate Directorship Practices: Membership & Committees of the Board.* In the Conference Board Report. #588, 1973.

BERLE, A. A., JR. "Economic Power and the Free Society." New York: The Fund for the Republic, Inc., 1957.

"Corporate Accountability Proposals of the Securities and Exchange Commission: A Time for Thoughtful Consideration," prepared by Peat, Marwick, Mitchell and Co., 1977.

Corporate Director's Guidebook, prepared by the Subcommittee on Functions and Responsibilities of Directors, of the Committee on Corporate Laws, Section of Corporation, Banking, and Business Law: American Bar Association, 1976.

"Foreign Corrupt Practices Act of 1977, an Overview of the Law and Its Implications," Ernst and Ernst, Financial Reporting Developments, February, 1978.

LEVITT, THEODORE. "The Dangers of Social Responsibility." *Harvard Business Review.* September-October, 1958.

LODGE, GEORGE; and MARTIN, WILLIAM. "Our Society in 1985, Business May Not Like it." *Harvard Business Review* (November-December 1975): 53 (no. 6), 143–152.

"OECD, Guidelines for Multinational Enterprises." Paris: The Organization for Economic Cooperation and Development, 1976.

SCHULTZE, CHARLES L. "The Public Use of Private Interest." *Harpers* 254, (May 1977): 43–62.

SIMON, WILLIAM E. "Getting Government Out of the Marketplace." *Saturday Review* (July 1975): 10–20.

.

Index

Index

Abrams, Frank W., quoted, 45
Abundance, material, 7, 13, 18, 142
Accountancy, 110
Adaptability, 138, 139, 142, 144
Adaptation, 32, 122, 142
    to aspirations and policies of host country, 135–37
    by boards of directors, 93–95
    by businessmen to change in values, 17–18
    to changing world economy, 134–35
    to emerging environment, 142
    required by multinational companies, 133
Allen, Frederick Lewis, 128
American Telephone & Telegraph Company, 68
Andrews, Kenneth R., quoted, 100
Anshen, Melvin, quoted, 12
Antitrust laws, 38, 67–70
Antitrust policy, 63–70
    effect of, on inflation, 70–71
Attitudes
    contemporary, 19, 29–30
    need for change in, 144

Audit, of management's performance, 94
Authoritarianism, 4
    in business, 59, 60
Authority, 116, 142
    lines of, 104–105
    sharing of, by corporate management, 9–10
    unquestioned, 143
    within corporations, 104–105

Berle, Adolph A., Jr., 53
Birthrate, U.S., 28
Blacks, on boards of directors, 48
Blumberg, Phillip I., quoted, 50
Board of Directors, 11–12, 49, 54, 88, 89, 143
    character of effective members of, 49
    composition of, 95
    constituencies of, 44–51
    discussions among members of, 97
    liability risks of members of, 93
    as a monitoring board, 93–94

153

Board of Directors (*Cont.*):
prerequisites of, for adaptation
to today's needs, 93
public interest a proper
concern to, 96–97
role of, in winning credibility,
92
specialized representatives on,
48–50
strengthened role for, 91–95
types of directors now needed,
96–97
a variety of views on societal
issues desirable for, 96
Bosworth, Barry, quoted, 109
Bottom line, 24, 87, 95, 144
Brazil, 123
Budget, concern for the
disadvantaged expressed in
federal, 73
social considerations in a
corporate operating, 111
Bureaucracy, 122, 126
costs to business of federal,
102–103
in government welfare
program, 102
Burson-Marsteller Report, quoted,
108–109
Business, private. *See also*
Corporation
adversary posture of
government toward, 43–44
confused attitude of, toward
regulation, 5–6
constraints of competition on,
40
a continuous flow of
transactions, 107
in contract with government,
115–16
costs to, of federal
bureaucracy, 102–103
credibility gap of, 100
disdain by, of behavior of
bureaucrats, 122–23
economic education by, 38–40

Business, private (*Cont.*):
education of public by, 43–44
government's distrust of, 122–
23
ill-prepared for some new
matters, 101
joint ventures of, with
government, 127
making the case today for,
124–26
need for change in structures
of administration of, 105–
106; for credibility, 92; to
involve itself, 111; for wise
participants in new
decisions, 111
new interests of, 107–108
new social responsibilities of,
26–27
operation of, by government,
128
participation in national
debates by, 108
poor fit of social commitment
and, 103
public criticism of, 37–38
relations with government,
119–29
social commitment of, called
for, 106–111
social effects of actions by, 113
supplier–customer relationship
of, to government, 126–28
traditional functions and work
of, 120–21, 124–26
world, 133–37
Businessmen
as consultants to government,
126–27
ethical behavior of, 57–58
public image of, 57, 58
Business Week, quoted, 134

Calvin, John, 20

Capital
  accumulation of, 25, 29
  formation of, 124
  mobility of, 41
Capitalism, new questionings
    about the performance of,
    24–25
Career progression, 116
Carson, Rachel, 108
Chairman of the board, 89, 91,
    94, 97–98
  as catalyst of consensus, 97
  as company spokesman, 94,
    97
  suggested corporate functions
    of, 99
Change(s)
  attitudinal, need for, 26–27
  in the evolution of the
    corporation, 10
  public demands for, 5
  in values and attitudes, 17
Charity, 19
Chief executive officer, 86–89,
    93–94
  new adjustments for, 87–88
  suggested operating functions
    of, 99
  vis-à-vis chairman of the
    board, 97–98
Church, values of medieval, 19
City Venture Corporation, 114
Clayton Act, 65, 71
  Cellar–Kefauver Amendment
    to, 66
Code of Federal Regulation, 103
Codes of conduct, 57, 60
Collaboration, xxii, 109, 113,
    116–17, 142
Collective bargaining, failure of,
    to relate wage adjustments
    to productivity, 74–75
Commission on Federal
    Paperwork, 102
Commitment, social, of business,
    106–111
Companies, joint stock, 20

Compassion, 19, 24, 31, 100, 142
  for the working man, 73
Competition, xxii, 6, 17, 22, 39–
    40, 43, 63, 64–65, 66, 67,
    69, 90, 104, 109, 116–17,
    134, 142
  adaptations to, in foreign
    countries, 139
  and antitrust policies, 64–70
  and antitrust protection of less
    efficient, 69, 70
  disciplining, 75–76
  economic, 38
  among managers, 117
  priority of security objectives
    over, 76
  protection of, 42
  "workable," 110
Conflicts of interests, 45–47
Conformity, 59
  within the company, 24
Consensus, xxii, 116, 142
Constituencies, of boards of
    directors, 44–51
Consumerism, 108–109
Consumer movement, 26
Consumer protection, 120, 123
Control Data Corporation, 114
Control systems, 104–105
Cooperation, 109, 116
"Co-production scheme," 138
Corporate law, 7–8, 83
Corporate structure, 104–106
  effect on, of interface between
    corporation and government,
    117–18
Corporation(s), 25, 81, 137. *See
    also* Business; Board of
    Directors
  adaptability of foreign
    affiliates of, 139
  adjustments required by, 11,
    33
  advisability of realigning
  · responsibilities within, 88
  affected by changes in values,
    32

Corporation(s) (*Cont.*):
basic legitimacy of, 7
as centrally important
institution, 142–43
concepts that have shaped, 18–
22
as conditioner of conduct of
officers, 59
constituency representation on
boards of, 44–51
contribution to a free society
of, 13–14
as efficient way to get
something done, 103
evolution of the modern, 18–22
flowering of the, 22–23
free-speech rights of, 108
future of, 144
as ill-equipped to make case
against inflation, 125
inadequacy of structure of
typical, 104–105
influence of, on daily life, 12–
13; on political institutions,
13
interlocking directors of, 45–
47
legal foundation of, 44
long-range interest as target of,
90
loss of freedom of action of, 14
model of purely economic, 82;
of socioeconomic, 83
multinational, 130–33, 135–
36, 137, 138, 139
need for changes in
administrative structures of,
105–106
need of, to be adaptive, 12, 92–
93, 108; to control unethical
practices, 60–61
new assignments of
responsibilities within, 111
new forms of foreign
investment by, 137–40
new problems of multinational,
139

Corporation(s) (*Cont.*):
one-man control of,
reexamined, 88–91
one-man vs. consensual control
of, 84–86
policy setting by, 92, 94
as purely profit-making
organization, 6–7
and public policy toward, 10–
12
public pressures at work on,
141–42
as a qualitatively complex
organization, 81–82
quasi-constituents of, 11–12
restructuring of, now needed,
17–18, 111–14
social responsibilities of, 6–7;
hazards therein, 8ff.
societal aspects of day-by-day
operations of, 113–15
status of, as "legal person," 22
strengthened role for board of,
91–95
as suppliers of armaments,
126
tasks ahead for, 105ff.
today's managers of, 37
transformation of, xx–xxii
in transition, 3ff.
typical organization of, 104–
106
use of task groups, 113
as vehicle for growth of
production, 23
Costs
labor, 75
rising, 31, 72, 73
social, 10–11; some shifted
onto corporations, 32
unit, 24, 32
"Creative man," 30
Credibility, of business, 92, 94,
100, 125
Currency
common, for Western Europe,
135

Currency (*Cont.*):
  maintenance of stability of,
    123–24

Darwin, Charles, 22
Decision makers, 104
Decision making, 8, 10, 33, 84, 85
  consensual, 95–98
Deficit financing, 72
  federal, 72, 73
Democracy, 13, 14
Directors
  interlocking, 45–47
  outside, 91
  special interest, 48–51
  women, blacks, and academics,
    95
Discrimination, against
  minorities, 101
Divestiture, suits seeking, 67, 68,
  69
Dividends, 54
Dollar, purchasing power of, 73
Doomsayers, 3

Eastman Kodak, 69
Ecology, 108, 109
"Economic man," 7, 30, 81, 142
Education, public economic, 38ff.
Efficiency, 6, 8, 17, 18, 24, 66, 96,
  100–101, 104, 142
Egalitarianism, xxi
Employment
  benefits, 31–32
  commitment to full, 71, 72
  training, 27
Energy
  policy, 122
  relative costs of, 133
Enlightened self-interest. *See*
  Self-interest

Environmental concerns, 101
Environmental protection, 27
Ethics, defined, 56

Fair trade laws, 76
Federal Trade Commission, 69,
  70
*First National Bank of Boston v.
  Pellotti*, 108
Flexibility, 32, 122
  needed in corporate response,
    106
Freedom, 21
Free enterprise, authoritarian in
  principle, 59
Free market, 41, 66, 82, 122, 125,
  143
  qualifications of, 76
Free society, 111
Fringe benefits, 71
Fulfillment, individual, 30
Full Employment Act of 1945, 71

General Motors Corp., 48, 114
Gerstacher, Carl A., quoted, 43
GNP (Gross National Product),
  11
  share of, taken by public
    services, 115
Government
  aversion of, to profit, 115
  bureaucratization of welfare
    program, 102
  business as an adversary of,
    5–6
  contract work for, 114–16
  customer–supplier relationship
    of, to business, 126–28
  disciplining of competition by,
    75–76
  distrust of business, 122–23

Government (*Cont.*):
encroachment of, on management, 9
functions within province of, 121–24
inadequacies of, in solving social ills, 101–103
joint task forces with business, 117–18; joint ventures, 127–28
and mercantilism, 20
posture toward business, 43–44
as producer and distributor, 13
relations with business, 119–29
as restraint on business, 26
shifting role of, 25–26
traditional functions of, 120
Government employment, 115
Governmental controls, 37
Governmental regulation, 39
Great Depression, 70
Greenleaf, Robert K., quoted, 88, 91
Growth, economic
changing rate of, 28–29
doubt as to future, 29
global, 134
idea of ever-expanding, 22
in less-developed countries, 134
maximum, 17

Harrington, Michael J., quoted, 141
Hauser, Theodore, quoted, 105
HEW (Health, Education and Welfare Department), 102
Humanism, 30, 128, 140, 142
values of, xxi–xxii, 17, 32

IBM (International Business Machines Corp.), 68, 69, 137

Ideology, emerging, 129
Incentives, 112, 123
Individualism, 142
Inflation, 65, 70–75, 125, 135
antitrust policy and, 70–71
built-in by national policies, 74–75
demands of labor and for social services as cause of, 74
rates of, 124
start of, 70
Influence payments, 57
Investment
international, 132–33
new forms of foreign, 137–40
Investment trusts, 47
Isaacs, Harold R., quoted, 25

Job training, 32
Joint venture, by multinationals, with host government, 137–38
Justice, 31

Kaplan, A. D. H., quoted, 75
Kappel, Frederick R., quoted, 5
Kings, divine right of, 25
Kissinger, Henry, quoted, 103, 133

Labor force
in U.S., 28
world, 136
Labor union pension funds, 47–48
Labor unions, exemption of, from antitrust laws, 70–71, 76

Legislation, constraining
    corporations, 7–8
Leisure, 30
Levitt, Theodore, quoted, 8
Liberalism, 42–43
Libertarianism, 22, 42–43
Liberty, natural, 24
Line and staff relationships, 117
Lippmann, Walter, 57
Locke, John, 21
Lockheed Aircraft, 126

Machiavelli, Niccolò di Bernardo
    20
Management (corporate), 5, 7–8,
    10, 143
  authoritative vs. consensual,
    84–86
  changed focus of purpose
    needed by, 14
  chief executive officer, 86–89
  consideration of constituents'
    varying interests by, 90–91
  contradictory socioeconomic
    pulls on, 83–84
  current dilemma of, 8–9, 143
  difficulties of, in social
    performance, 27
  of multinational companies,
    136
  optimum policies for, 144
  perception of social
    implications of decisions by,
    10–11
  quasi-constituencies of, 7–8,
    11–12, 56
  relationships of, with
    stockholders, 54–55
  responsiveness of, to public 53;
    to stockholders, 52
  role of, vis-à-vis board of
    directors, 91–92, 94–95
  slowness of, in adapting to
    public attitudes, 26
  use of task groups, 113

Management contract, 138
Manager, professional, 53–54
Managers, 7, 142
Manhattan Project, 114
Market system, 11, 13–14. *See
    also* Free market
Markets, changing, 105
Materialism, 142
Matrix management, 113, 116
McCracken, Paul W., quoted, 75
Means, Gardiner, 53
Mercantilism, 20, 21
Mergers, 64, 65, 66
Mexico, 123
Miller–Tydings Act of 1937, 69–
    70
*Modern Corporation and Private
    Property, The,* 53
Monarchy, 19–20, 21
Monetary policy, 72
Monopoly, 39, 64, 65, 138–39
Motivation, 100, 112, 117
Moynihan, Daniel P., quoted, 13
Multinational companies, 130–
    33, 135–36, 137, 138, 139

Nader, Ralph, 108
NASA (National Aeronautics and
    Space Administration), 114
Nationalism, economic, 131–
    32
Nature, 20–21
  lack of reverence for, 19
  as something to be exploited,
    23
Natural sciences, values of, 32
Newton, Isaac, 20
New York City, 127
New York Times, quoted, 137
NRA (National Recovery Act),
    57

Okun, Arthur M., quoted, 46

Open market, *See* Free market
Opportunity, equality of, 11
Organization, corporate, need for
    modification of, 111ff., 115–
    16

Parity prices, 76
Payments
    illegal domestic, 54
    influence, 57
    off-book, 58, 60
    undisclosed foreign, 54
Pension funds, 47–48
Pensions, 27, 31, 55
Performance, audit of, 94
Personnel, policies and practices
    regarding, 30–31, 94, 135–
    36, 139
Pertschuk, Michael, quoted, 66
Planning, long-term strategic,
    111, 112
Plant safety, 123
Policies, of multinationals, 138–
    39
Policy making, 92, 94, 98
Politics, 124–25
Pollution, 27, 101, 122
Population trends
    in less-developed countries,
    136
    in U.S., 28
Power, ultimate source of, 21, 25
Price behavior, 41, 42, 66, 70,
    73, 83
Price controls, 22
Price level, 75
Price maintenance, 64–65
Prices
    higher, resulting from
        increased wages, 72
    relative, function of, 41
Procedures, overview of, 94
Production
    increased efficiency of, 100–
    101
    large-scale, 13

Productivity, 71, 74, 75, 124
    and federal regulations, 103
Profitability, 18, 96, 110
Profit centers, 104
Profit-making, 130
Profits, 38, 39–40, 59
    economic function of, 40–41
    maximizing, 5, 33, 81
    purpose of a corporation, 6–7
Project management, 113, 116
Project task forces, 117
Property, private, 22, 23
Proxy machinery, 54
"Psychological man," 30
Public interest, 108, 122, 125
    groups, 54
"Public man," 30
Puritans, 19, 20, 30

Quality-of-life, concerns and
    considerations, 9–10, 31, 87,
    101, 114, 120, 121, 128
Quasi-constituencies, of
    corporate management, 7–8,
    11–12, 56, 83
Quotas, 135

Randall, Clarence, quoted, 59,
    143
Rate of return, 39–40
Rationality, xxi–xxii, 17, 128
Raw materials, 134
Record-keeping, 32
Redevelopment, urban, 114, 127
Reformation, 19
Regulation, governmental, of
    business, 5, 9, 10, 121–22,
    123, 125–26
Relationships, business-
    government, 119–29
Religion, xxi, xxii
"Religious man," 30

Renaissance, 19
Research and development, 105
Responsibility, in typical
    corporate structure, 104
Responsibilities
    new social, of business, 6–7,
      26–27
    organizing for enlarged social,
      111–14, 116–18
Restraints, external political, 24
Retirees, 31–32
Retirement policy, questions of,
    30–31
Right to strike, 71
Robinson–Patman Act of 1936,
    69
Rostow, Eugene, quoted, 11

Science, xxi–xxii, 20–21, 23, 142
    values of, 140
SCM vs. Xerox, 67–68
SEC (Securities and Exchange
    Commission), 51
Security
    given priority by government
      over free competition, 75–
      76
    personal, 29–30, 32
    within a corporation, 59
Self-interest, enlightened, 22, 38,
    81, 107
Self-regulation, of business, 123,
    125–26
Self-reliance, xxii, 21, 29, 110,
    120, 142
Self-restraint, 58, 60–61
Senate Commerce Committee, 51
Shenafield, John H., quoted, 68
Sherman Act, 65, 70
Singapore, 123
Smith, Adam, 21, 81, 82
Social commitment, of business,
    109–110
Social contract, 21, 25

Social issues, devices to develop
    company awareness of,
    111–12
Social responsibility, new, of
    business today, 27, 28
Social services, financial
    requirements of, today, 115
Society
    changes within, 4–5
    ills of, today, 101
    influence of the corporation
      on, 13
    interests of, 82, 83
South Korea, 123
Special interest groups, 12
Spokesmen, business, 18
Stewardship, 19, 53
Stockholder democracy, 51–55,
    56
    and public attitudes, 53
Stockholders, 7, 10, 11, 14, 45,
    56, 82, 89, 90, 91, 107, 108
    dissenting minority, 55
    relationships of, with
      management, 54–55
    use of proxy by minority
      groups of, 54
Stock options, 55
Structure, administrative, 113,
    130, 139
Subsidies, 42

Tariffs, 76
Task groups, 113
Tax ceiling, 115
Taxes, 73, 124, 125
Technology, 13, 23, 74, 105
Thailand, 123
Thrift, 19, 30
Trade, international, 130, 132,
    134
Trade-offs, 75, 110
Transfer payments, 132
Transportation, 128
Trilling, Lionel, quoted, 43

Underemployment, 28, 31
Underutilization, of abilities, 31
Unemployment, 29, 74
Unit costs, of production, 71, 72, 75, 110, 124, 126
Urban rehabilitation, 114

Values. *See also* Attitudes
God-centered, 16
inversion of social, 19–20
of libertarian society, 32
man-centered, 16
medieval, out of favor, 19–20
national structure of, 120–21
non-economic, 10
rearrangement of, 25
shifting of people's, today, 15–17
of society, 6, 10, 142, 144

Vinci, Leonardo da, quoted, 23, 32

Wages, 71, 72
of employees of multinationals, 135
and inflationary settlements, 73–75
Wagner Act of 1935, 71
Walton, Clarence C., quoted, 129
Wealth, 19
Adam Smith's view of, 21–22
Weaver, Paul, quoted, 42
Welfare, 102, 120
costs of, 73
Western Electric, 68
"Whole man," the, 142
Work, as a means of self-expression, 31
World economy, 130

PROGRAM FOR STUDIES OF
THE MODERN CORPORATION
Graduate School of Business, Columbia University

PUBLICATIONS

FRANCIS JOSEPH AGUILAR
Scanning the Business Environment

MELVIN ANSHEN, *editor*
Managing the Socially Responsible Corporation

HERMAN W. BEVIS
Corporate Financial Reporting in a Competitive Economy

COURTNEY C. BROWN
Beyond the Bottom Line

COURTNEY C. BROWN
Putting the Corporate Board to Work

COURTNEY C. BROWN, *editor*
World Business: Promise and Problems

CHARLES DE HOGHTON, *editor*
The Company: Law, Structure, and Reform

RICHARD EELLS
The Corporation and the Arts

RICHARD EELLS, *editor*
International Business Philanthropy

RICHARD EELLS and CLARENCE WALTON, *editors*
Man in the City of the Future

JAMES C. EMERY
*Organizational Planning and Control Systems:
Theory and Technology*

ALBERT S. GLICKMAN, CLIFFORD P. HAHN, EDWIN A. FLEISHMAN, and BRENT BAXTER
Top Management Development and Succession: An Exploratory Study

NEIL H. JACOBY
Corporate Power and Social Responsibility

NEIL H. JACOBY
Multinational Oil: A Study in Industrial Dynamics

NEIL H. JACOBY, PETER NEHEMKIS, and RICHARD EELLS
Bribery and Extortion in World Business: A Study of Corporate Political Payments Abroad

JAY W. LORSCH
Product Innovation and Organization

KENNETH G. PATRICK
Perpetual Jeopardy—The Texas Gulf Sulphur Affair: A Chronicle of Achievement and Misadventure

KENNETH G. PATRICK and RICHARD EELLS
Education and the Business Dollar

IRVING PFEFFER, *editor*
The Financing of Small Business: A Current Assessment

STANLEY SALMEN
Duties of Administrators in Higher Education

GEORGE A. STEINER
Top Management Planning

GEORGE A. STEINER and WILLIAM G. RYAN
Industrial Project Management

GEORGE A. STEINER and WARREN M. CANNON, *editors*
Multinational Corporate Planning

GUS TYLER
The Political Imperative: The Corporate Character of Unions

CLARENCE WALTON and RICHARD EELLS, *editors*
The Business System: Readings in Ideas and Concepts

Courtney C. Brown

DR. COURTNEY C. BROWN is Dean Emeritus and Paul Garrett Emeritus Professor of Public Policy and Business Responsibility of the Graduate School of Business of Columbia University. He is a recent Chairman of the Board of Directors of the American Assembly.

Born in 1904, in St. Louis, Missouri, he was educated at Dartmouth College and did graduate work in economics at Columbia University. During World War II, he served with the Department of State and the War Food Administration in negotiations with other countries to procure their exportable surpluses of supplies needed by the Allies. Following the war, he was associated with the Standard Oil Company (New Jersey) as Chief Petroleum Economist and Assistant to the Chairman of the Board.

Dr. Brown has had long personal experience with the boards of both business and charitable corporations. He has served on the boards of directors of Esso Standard Oil Company, American Standard, American Electric Power, the Borden Company, Uris Buildings, and the New York Stock Exchange. At the present, he serves on the boards of Associated Dry Goods, the Columbia Broadcasting System, Union Pacific Corporation, and the West Side Advisory Board of the Chemical Bank. He serves on the Executive Committee of two of these companies, and as Chairman of the Audit Committee of another, the Conflict of Interests Committee of a second, and the Executive Compensation Committee of a third.

His experience on the boards of not-for-profit corporations is equally wide, having served on the boards of the Interracial Council for Business Opportunity and the New York Advisory Board of the Salvation Army. Currently, he is a member of the boards of the American Assembly, and the Academy of Political Science. He is an honorary director of the Council for Financial Aid to Education (which he assisted Alfred P. Sloan, Irving Olds, and Frank W. Abrams to found in 1952).